TABLE

Acknowledgements	vii
Dedication	ix
Introduction	1
A Theology of Marriage	13
What Went Wrong?	29
Common Areas of Disagreement	47
Spouse Hunting Part 1	81
Spouse Hunting Part 2	123
How to be a Biblical Husband Part 1	157
How to be a Biblical Husband Part 2	193
How to be a Biblical Wife Part 1	207
How to be a Biblical Wife Part 2	233
Closing Thoughts and Encouragements	257
Scripture Index	263
About the Author	267

Made in United States
Orlando, FL
25 September 2024

Til Death Do Us Part

TIL DEATH DO US PART

A Grace-Based Approach to Dating and Marriage

John Thomas Clark, ThM, DMin
Tetelestai Press

Til Death Do Us Part: A Grace-Based Approach to Dating and Marriage
© 2022 Copyright by John Thomas Clark
Published by Tetelestai Press

No part of this publication may be reproduced, stored in a retrieval system, or transmitted in any form or by any means, electronic, mechanical, photocopying, recording, scanning, or otherwise, except as permitted under Section 107 or 108 of the 1976 United States Copyright Act, without the prior written permission of the Publisher. Requests to the Publisher for permissions should be sent to Tetelestai Press, john316clarkie@gmail.com

ISBN: 978-1-7353359-6-4

ACKNOWLEDGEMENTS

"Til Death Do Us Part" was born out of a desire to provide a helpful tool for those who ARE married, those who ARE GETTING married, and those who HOPE TO MARRY someday. It is written with the person in mind who desires their marriage to thrive and NOT just survive. This study is designed to be a multi-purpose interactive tool that can be used on a personal level, in small group studies, for pre-marital counseling, or even marital counseling.

Much of what is shared in these pages is born out of failure. Both the failure of others, and the author's own failure in marriage. There is nothing like thinking something is easy and will come naturally, and then finding yourself on your knees time and time again. Then after failing, apologizing, and promising "never to do _____" again – doing it all over again and repeating the cycle.

The goal of the book is to mix biblical truth from a grace-based perspective with practical advice. As in everything in our Christian lives, the goal of the book is to emphasize with no apologies the absolute necessity of depending upon Jesus Christ and Him alone for the resources to be the type of spouse you want to be. This book heavily emphasizes the grace of God, the finished work of Jesus Christ for our deliverance from sin's power, and the empowering work of the Holy Spirit as absolute necessities for a God-honoring marriage. Make no mistake – in order to be the spouse, we need to be biblically, we must rely upon God to deliver us from the indwelling power of sin in our lives.

Again, my prayer was to create a tool that is replicable and easy to study with someone else! May your marriage and your response to your role in marriage bring God all the glory He desires from it.

By His Grace,
John Clark, Thm, DMin

DEDICATION

First and foremost, I give God all the praise and glory for His faithfulness in exposing me to sound Bible teaching in my life. Each day, I rejoice more in the finished work of Jesus Christ, and I am thankful for the men who have taught me clearly of the wonderful work of my Savior. This is true, not only in the area of justification, but also in the area of sanctification. For that, I am eternally grateful!

I am grateful to my wife, Carrie, my best friend in life. She has truly blessed me beyond words by simply saying "yes" to my proposal of marriage many years ago. Next to trusting Jesus Christ as my Savior, marrying Carrie was the best decision I have ever made. She has supported me in so many different ways in our marriage, and I cannot say enough words to express the honor and love I have for her. Even with this book project, she functioned as my unofficial "grammar policewoman" in the writing process, and she provided her unending love, support, and encouragement! She even provided some comic relief, as I got notes from her throughout the manuscript process ribbing me (lovingly) about the disparity between my teaching and my execution of it practically! Touché, hon!

I am so thankful for my kids (Abby, Cody, Riley, Sadie, and Tobin), who are beautiful blessings from Carrie's and my union, and who are huge motivators for me. I love you, kids, and pray God prepares you and each of your potential future spouses for thriving marriages — marriages where each of you and your spouses build each other up and support one another to become all that Jesus Christ has designed you to be. I pray that each and every day of your lives that you see the value of what Jesus did for you!

My parents, Larry and Kathy Clark, who raised me in a Christian home and shared the gospel with me at five-years-old. I am eternally grateful to you both! My Dad passed away in 2019 from Alzheimer's Dementia, but he was truly one of the best friends I ever had. My Mom is still my number one fan (or #2 next to my wife) even after all the grief I put her through as a teenager!

A special thanks to Emily Miller, my administrative assistant, who made this project a reality with her work in formatting these manuscripts into book form.

Another special thanks to the following men who agreed to read through and provide critique of the manuscript at different stages along the way: Robert Ambs, Ken Draper, Jeremy Jackson, and Rob Armstrong.

Also, a special thanks to my current leadership board at Grace Community Fellowship in Newnan, Georgia. These men are huge supporters of any project or idea that further promotes grace and healthy marriages and families! I so appreciate working with them!

A special thanks to the couples that Carrie and I have had the pleasure of working with in pre-marital counseling during our time in Newnan, Georgia. Thanks to: Leonard and Julia, Joseph and Rachel, Paul and Becka, Alex and Autumn, and Tyler and Jenna. Carrie and I continue to pray for your marriages, and we want God's best for you! Christ is enough for each one of you!

CHAPTER 1
INTRODUCTION

There it is in black ink – basic requirements: (1) Applicants must be at least sixteen years of age, (2) Applicants must have held an Instructional Permit (CP) for a minimum of one year and a day, (3) Applicants cannot have any major traffic violations that resulted in the suspension of the Instructional Permit, (4) Applicants must have a minimum of forty hours of supervised driving experience with at least six hours of driving at night, (5) Applicants must pass a vision exam, (6) Applicants must be prepared to take the applicable Road Skills Test, (7) Applicants under eighteen are required to have a parent/guardian, responsible adult or authorized driver training instructor sign the application for the driver's license, and Applicants must pay thirty-two dollars. These are the requirements for obtaining a Georgia's State Driver's License.[1]

---

[1] Author Unknown, "How Do I Get My First Driver's License?," Georgia Department of Driver Services, accessed July 1, 2020, https://dds.georgia.gov/how-do-i-class-d.

In contrast, consider the following basic requirements for obtaining a marriage license in the Georgia county of residence of the author. (1) Applicants must be at least eighteen years of age, (2) Applicants must fill out the appropriate paperwork, (3) Applicants must pay a fifty-six-dollar fee, unless they have taken a qualifying premarital education program, and then they only have to pay a sixteen-dollar fee.[2] By comparing the basic requirements of each, it appears twice as hard to get a driver's license in the state of Georgia, then it is to get a marriage license in the same state. Some may say that driving is more dangerous than getting married, but I disagree. In fact, I would say that a marriage "gone wrong" is one of the most dangerous things that can happen in people's lives today. Damaged and destroyed marriages lead to all sorts of lingering problems in society, governments, churches, and individual lives.

This book is NOT primarily written with the unbeliever in mind. I do believe that unbelievers can benefit from some of the truths in this book,

---

[2] Author Unknown, "Marriage Licenses," Coweta County, accessed July 1, 2020, https://www.coweta.ga.us/government/courts/probate-2020/marriage-licenses#:~:text=If%20the%20couple%20has%20completed,use%20of%20a%20charge%20card.).

but ultimately unbelievers or seekers need to hear ONE message and ONE message only, and that is the gospel of Jesus Christ. That message is a simple, yet often confused, message that simply states the Jesus Christ died for our sins and rose again on the third day (1 Corinthians 15:3-4). The reason this message is such good news is because each one of us has sinned or broken God's Law (Romans 3:23). The consequence of breaking God's Law is death and hell (Romans 6:23a). God did not want anyone to go to hell, which is why He sent His only begotten Son to die for us, in our place, so that we would never have to face this death penalty on our own (Romans 5:8). In this death, Jesus Christ paid in full the entire penalty for each one of our sins (John 19:30). The response God requires of each man, woman, and child in order to benefit from Jesus' accomplishment on the cross is to BELIEVE that Jesus Christ died and rose again for his or her sins (Acts 16:31). It is NOT by walking an aisle, praying a prayer, committing or surrendering one's life to Him, turning from all one's sins, promising to follow Him, asking Him into one's heart, etc. It is through simple reliance upon what Jesus did for each one of us, NOT relying upon something we must do for Him. For a video presentation of this same message, please visit:

https://www.youtube.com/c/GraceCommunityFellowshipChurch

And watch the video entitled "The Most Amazing Message in the World".

Moreover, this book is written with believers in mind because the teaching contained therein is solely based upon the divine resources that are available only to those who are IN Christ. These resources include many things, more than can be named, but specifically God's solution for delivering us from sin's power and God's very presence in us via the Holy Spirit. Without the work of Jesus Christ accomplished TO us through our co-crucifixion and co-resurrection WITH Him and the Spirit's execution of deliverance from sin's power as we walk by faith, we have absolutely no chance at a God-honoring marriage.

Now, to set the stage for our study, it is important to recognize some divine institutions that God Himself has established for an organized, fruitful society. These divine institutions are the most fundamental and basic practices that God has set up for the human race in order to protect them, preserve them, and allow them to enjoy blessings on earth to their fullest. It is in and through these divine institutions that God allows human beings to enjoy and pursue things with eternal benefit and value while living on this earth. These divine institutions are the following: marriage, family, government, and the local church. Therefore, if I am thinking like God's enemy, which divine institution should I attack to give me the most bang for my buck? Which divine institution, if crumbled, would have the greatest negative effects on society? Clearly, the answer would be marriage because it is the "building block" for things, such as child-rearing, society, government, and the local church. The late Dr. Charles Ryrie stated:

> The Word of God has nothing to say about organizing a Sunday school, a Youth for Christ or Young Life group, a Christian day school or college, a seminary, or about publishing Christian books or magazines; yet no one denies the importance of these means in accomplishing the Lord's work, and no one considers them unscriptural in any sense. But the word of God has much to say about organizing and running a Christian home. When will Christians realize the importance of obeying this part of God's revelation to us,

not only for what it would mean to our homes but also for what it would mean to all aspects of God's work in the earth?[3]

This is precisely why, I believe, marriage as a whole is under attack and is a **primary target** by our three enemies: the world, the flesh, and the devil. Consider the following statistics:

1. In the United States, there is one divorce approximately every thirty-six seconds, which translates to 2,400 divorces per day, 16,800 divorces per week, and 876,000 divorces per year.[4] This means that there are approximately eighty-three divorces during a typical Sunday sermon. Thus, the United States has the highest divorce rate in the world!

2. Women initiate divorce twice as often as men.[5]

---

[3] Charles Ryrie, "Is Your Home Scriptural?," *Galaxie Software Publishing*, accessed August 23, 2020, https://www.galaxie.com/article/bsac109-436-07.

[4] Author Unknown, "32 Shocking Divorce Statistics," accessed November 4, 2020, last modified October 30, 2012, https://www.mckinleyirvin.com/family-law-blog/2012/october/32-shocking-divorce-statistics/.

[5] Kathleen O'Connell Corcoran, "Psychological and Emotional Aspects of Divorce," accessed November 4, 2020, last modified June 1997, https://www.mediate.com/articles/psych.cfm.

3. Social Media Stats on Divorce: one in three divorces start as online affairs.[6] 25% of couples fight about Facebook (or other social media platforms) at least once a week.[7] One in seven married people have contemplated divorce because of their partner's social media activity.[8] One in five married people feel uneasy about their relationship after discovering something on their partner's Facebook account.[9] Facebook is the number one source for online divorce evidence.[10] 81% of AAML divorce attorneys have used or encountered evidence obtained from social media.[11] 14% of adults say they look through their partner's social media accounts for evidence of infidelity.[12]

---

[6] "32 Shocking Divorce Statistics," https://www.mckinleyirvin.com/family-law-blog/2012/october/32-shocking-divorce-statistics/.
[7] Ibid.
[8] Ibid.
[9] Ibid.
[10] Ibid.
[11] Ibid.
[12] Ibid.

4. Percent of marriages where one or both spouses admit to infidelity, either physical or emotional is 41%.[13] However, the percentage of men who said they would have an affair if they knew they would never get caught was 74%, and the number of women was 68%.[14]

5. A newer phenomenon catching many adherents is known as **Gray** Divorce, meaning divorce among those aged 54-64. In this group, the divorce rate has quadrupled over the past thirty years – one in four divorces in 2010 involved couples age fifty and older, compared to one in ten in 1990.[15]

6. Ironically enough, divorce is actually on the decline in the United States. In the 1980's, 50% of every marriage (Christian or non-Christian) ended in divorce. This is where we get the often used

---

[13] Author Unknown, "These Cheating Statistics Probably Hit Close to Home (Statistically)," Newswire, accessed July 1, 2020, last modified April 22, 2014, https://www.newswire.com/these-cheating-statistics-probably/271424.
[14] "These Cheating Statistics Probably Hit Close to Home (Statistically)," https://www.newswire.com/these-cheating-statistics-probably/271424.
[15] "32 Shocking Divorce Statistics," https://www.mckinleyirvin.com/family-law-blog/2012/october/32-shocking-divorce-statistics/.

50% number, but the most recent statistics put that number closer to 40%.[16][17]

Considering the fact that divorce is on the decline, should we be happy? Unfortunately, no, this statistic is necessarily good news. There are outliers in statistics, variables that are hard to account for. One such outlier or variable in the marriage and divorce statistics is the practice of COHABITATION. Cohabitation is skewing the ability to compare all previous marriage statistics. Cohabitation is defined as living together **without** being married, and it is on the rise. It subscribes to *worldly wisdom,* which goes something like this: "We are in love with each other, and we want to get married someday, but we feel like it would be wise and prudent to try it out first, just in case we are seeing it wrong now. Then, if we need to call it off, it will not be a messy divorce." One of the many tragic

---

[16] Belinda Luscombe, "The Divorce Rate is Dropping. That May Not Actually Be Good News," accessed November 4, 2020, last modified November 26, 2018, https://time.com/5434949/divorce-rate-children-marriage-benefits/.

[17] This just represents the number of marriages that end in divorce and DOES NOT measure the percentage of marriages that are just barely surviving and on life support. If 40% of the marriages end in divorce, it is very naïve to assume that 60% of the marriages are strong and healthy. I am not sure what my guess would be if put in a corner, but my answer would probably not be too positive considering the amount of serious marital issues that come across my desk as a pastor.

outcomes of cohabitation is that women (as a general rule) are more likely to see cohabitation as the next logical step in their relationship, whereas men (as a general rule) are more likely to see it as a compromise (i.e., it's less of a commitment than marriage). Even the joint decision to cohabit does not mean that couples are on the same page, as one may view it as a BIG commitment, and the other one may view it as a DELAY in commitment. Consider the following statistics regarding co-habitation:

1. Today, as many as 70% of women aged 30-34 have cohabited with a male partner.[18]
2. A 2016 Barna study revealed that the majority of Americans (65%) now believe that cohabitation before marriage is a good idea.[19]

---

[18] Steve Warren, "Study: Couples Who Live Together Before Marriage Are at Greater Risk of Divorce," accessed November 4, 2020, last modified October 22, 2018, https://www1.cbn.com/cbnnews/us/2018/october/study-couples-who-live-together-before-marriage-are-at-greater-risk-of-divorce-nbsp.

[19] George Barna, "Majority of Americans Now Believe in Cohabitation," accessed November 4, 2020, last modified June 24, 2016, https://www.barna.com/research/majority-of-americans-now-believe-in-cohabitation/.

3. Especially disturbing in this study is the conclusion that 41% percent of practicing Christians strongly or somewhat strongly agree that cohabitation is a good idea.[20]

4. The social science data on cohabitation is **very clear**: cohabitation leads to higher divorce rates after marriage. Even though this is the case, 81% of women who cohabit believe it will prevent future divorce.[21] It is clear that cohabitation does not fireproof your marriage, but rather throws gasoline and a match to it.

5. "People with cohabiting experience who marry have a 50 to 80% higher likelihood of divorcing than married couples who never cohabited."[22]

6. Researchers at UCLA found that cohabiters experienced significantly more difficulty in their marriages with adultery,

---

[20] Barna, "Majority of Americans Now Believe in Cohabitation."
[21] Colleen N. Nugent, Jill Daugherty, "A Demographic, Attitudinal, and Behavioral Profile of Cohabiting Adults in the United States, 2011-2015," *National Health Statistics Reports* Volume 111, May 31, 2018, 3.
[22] Brett Kunkle and John Stonestreet, A Practical Guide to Culture: Helping the Next Generation Navigate Today's World, (David C. Cook: Colorado Springs, 2017), 173.

alcohol, drugs, and domestic violence than couples who did not cohabit.[23]

7. In fact, 60% of young adults PLAN to cohabit before they marry.[24] What is the main reason as to why they pursue this course of action? It is because of the fact that their parents got divorced, and they think by cohabiting they will prevent divorce from happening to them.

If we are NOT personally grounded in biblical teaching on marriage and the family, there is NO HOPE for a lasting marriage. No amount of self-reliant and worldly strategy can insulate us from the pitfalls and rough patches that a marriage will inevitably face. In fact, all these other issues in marriage will be reduced to mere gnats yapping at our heels if we will **BUY IN** to God's plan for marriage and **RELY UPON** His resources to function in our roles. In fact, this is what this book is designed for – to encourage individuals to do marriage God's way and with His resources.

---

[23] Kunkle, "A Practical Guide to Culture," 173.
[24] Bill Maier, "Is Living Together a Good Test for Marital Compatibility?" accessed November 4, 2020, last modified January 1, 2008, https://www.focusonthefamily.com/marriage/dr-bill-maier-on-cohabitation/.

In addition, we need to be convinced of the BIBLICAL TRUTH that God has designed marriage to be the most elegant, satisfying expression of all possible relationships between people. As one author states, "God made marriage good. No, that's not emphatic enough. He made marriage much better than good. He made it to be terrific. And don't ever let our blurring of the picture, or your own self-doubts, keep you from discovering that for yourselves. Whenever God's promises are involved, it's worth a whole lifetime of hard work."[25] So, with that as an introduction, let's dive in!

---

[25] Joel Belz, "That's What He Meant – Great Expectations: God Makes Terrific Marriages," World Magazine, accessed January 6, 2021, last modified July 27, 2002, https://world.wng.org/2002/07/thats_what_he_meant.

CHAPTER 2
A THEOLOGY OF MARRIAGE

An often-used analogy in Christian circles is that the way to recognize counterfeit currency is by studying genuine currency. Bankers and treasury agents are indeed trained just as the analogy says - they do not bother to handle counterfeits, only real money and a lot of it. A treasury agent does not bother to study lists of known counterfeiting techniques because such information would be incomplete, or it would soon be outdated. In contrast, a treasury agent is steeped in the real thing, so he may know the weight, appearance, and smell of a real dollar bill. Thus, any new deception a counterfeiter throws at him can be immediately detected.[26] In much the same way, it is best to view the topic of marriage through the lens of God's original design for marriage. To do that, let's turn to Genesis chapter two and see WHY, HOW, and WHAT God did as it relates to establishing marriage as a divine institution for mankind's good.

---

[26] Tobin Duty, "Counterfeit Bills," Classical Conversations, accessed July 2, 2020, last modified April 5, 2012, https://members.classicalconversations.com/article/counterfeit-bills.

In order to summarize God's design for marriage, there are four main terms to understand from Genesis two. The four main terms are the following: Dependent, Oneness, Intimacy, and Transparency. It was pointed out to me that these four terms form an unfortunate acronym – D.O.I.T., (i.e., "Do It!" – Any Nike fans out there?) Although this acronym may indeed help us remember the summary terms, it is unfortunate because "Just Do-ing It" is the furthest thing from the true Biblical instruction for marriage. "Just Do It" is taken straight out of the legalistic playbook of "You just need to TRY harder," "You just need to BUCK UP," and "You just need to do THIS and stop doing THAT." In summary, the legalist would say, "You just need to TRUST yourself to DELIVER yourself, and you need to do this to be a better spouse." However, as we move through this study, it will become clear that this is the antithesis of grace and the exact opposite of how God would have us respond in our marriages.

DEPENDENT

Genesis 2:18-20 reads, "And the LORD God said, '*It is* not good that man should be alone; I will make him a helper comparable to him.' Out of the ground the LORD God formed every beast of the field and every bird of the air and brought *them* to Adam to see what he would call them. And whatever Adam called each living creature, that *was* its name. So, Adam gave names to all cattle, to the birds of the air, and to every beast of the field. But for Adam there was not found a helper comparable to him." Notice that the first thing that God says in verse 18 is that it is NOT GOOD that man should be alone." All of God's creation up to this point had been "good" and "very good!" In fact, at this point in Genesis that word and phrase had been used eight times. This is the first time in recorded human history that God says something is NOT GOOD! The situation that God identifies as NOT GOOD is "That man should be alone." Now, God has a remedy for this problem, but it is interesting to note that for some reason, God created man to need others, specifically in this case - **a spouse**. It is fascinating to consider that the all-knowing and infinitely loving Creator created man complete and yet incomplete at the same time with built-in NEEDS. Even though God was meeting all of Adam's needs personally, one NEED had been strikingly absent and unmet. Ironically enough, if God had not intervened, Adam may not have even known.

Notice **WHO** initiates this process – it is GOD who initiates and is pro-active, NOT man. Thus, marriage is a creation of God, designed to accomplish something for the benefit of mankind. God, being the Creator, knows what is best for His creatures, and He alone knows how to meet our needs. This is a principle that all mankind needs to grasp – God wants to meet ALL your needs. This is true in the area of the penalty of sin. God met our need by providing Jesus to die for our sin and rise again and to pay our sin debt penalty in full. Moreover, this is true in the area of the power of sin in our daily lives. God identified believers with Jesus in His death TO sin and resurrection to newness of life in order to free us from sin's power. In the area of dependency and need for companionship, God provided the institution of marriage. Unfortunately, for many of us, we try to meet our own needs, which is where we get into trouble.

Consider some of the miracles in nature and how God meets our NEEDS with different aspects of His creation. One such simple example is the honeybee, and the role it plays in our everyday lives. Bees give us a lot more than delicious honey. They are pollinators - they enable plants to produce the fruits and nuts we enjoy by carrying pollen from one plant or flower to the next. The wind pollinates oats, corn, and wheat, but many other plants (like apple trees, cherry trees, and melon vines) depend on insects, bats, and birds. Animals pollinate about one out of every three bites of food we eat. In the United States, millions and millions of bees, kept by human beekeepers, fly around doing a lot of this important work for food crops. Professional beekeepers raise honeybees, box them up, and send them on trucks to fields where farmers grow food. Bees live in groups of about 40,000 called colonies. In fact, California's almond crop alone depends on about half the bees in the country, about 1.5 million colonies! The bees pollinate in the almond groves for about six weeks and then are sent on to work other crops.[27]

Thus, it is clear that God knows what He is doing, and He knows exactly how to accomplish meeting our needs. It is interesting to consider that part of the reason Adam may have named the animals, in verses 19-20, was because God was showing him his NEED. As each animal had its

---

[27] Author Unknown, "Honeybee," National Geographic Kids, accessed July 2, 2020, http://kids.nationalgeographic.com/kids/stories/animalsnature/honey-bee-mystery/.

corresponding partner, Adam may have begun to realize he had no partner that corresponded to him. According to God's infinite wisdom, maybe this is HOW He introduced the concept of Adam's own NEED to himself because when one realizes their own need, he or she can genuinely appreciate the provision for his or her need. Now, we must be clear, Eve was not capable of meeting "ALL" of Adam's needs, nor was she designed that way. Rather, she would meet some of Adam's needs on this earth, and God would handle the rest in His own way. Also, it is good to note at this juncture that Adam was not capable of meeting "ALL" the woman's needs either. Even with God's design of marriage, God is always in the picture to be the ultimate "Need-meeter" for both husband and wife.

So, going back to the NOT GOOD situation that God identified, we see that God's solution is to make Adam a helper. This word "helper" means an assistant, or one who assists and serves another with what is needed; they provide acts of supplying what is needed to another.[28]

---

[28] James Swanson, Dictionary of Biblical Languages With Semantic Domains : Hebrew (Old Testament) (Oak Harbor:Logos Research Systems, Inc., 1997), Electronic ed., 6469.

A Theology of Marriage

"Helper" is used 280 times in 135 verses in the Old Testament. This word is used of God Himself multiple times in the Scriptures (Psalm 30:10; 33:20, etc.), and so it does not imply a "demeaning" or "inferior" position but rather implies a position of great value in meeting the needs of others! The type of helper that God provides for Adam is described as "comparable," meaning a counterpart, or an object which is corresponding or like another object. Thus, God describes man's "helper" as someone who is able to meet the needs that only someone with similar (i.e. same nature), yet different parts could supply. It is this very unity that would "complement" one another.[29]

God, knowing exactly what Adam needs in terms of a helper and knowing exactly how to provide this helper, now takes charge! Verses 21-22 state, "And the LORD God caused a deep sleep to fall on Adam, and he slept; and He took one of his ribs, and closed up the flesh in its place. Then the rib which the LORD God had taken from man He made into a woman,

---

[29] As a side note, notice that the woman's main role in a marriage is as a comparable helper to her husband…not a child-bearer. Women can be complete without bearing children.

and He brought her to the man." Notice, it is God who causes a deep sleep to fall on Adam; it is God who took one of Adam's ribs; it is God who closed up the flesh in its place; it is God who made the rib into a woman; and it is God who brought the woman to Adam. In fact, Adam had no part in this process, and he had no say. Adam merely **rested** - Adam's works had no part in obtaining a partner. Eve was totally a gift of God's grace. It is also valuable to note that Eve was taken from Adam's side, not his head or his foot. This, too, provides another strong image of her role as a companion or helper, not an inferior.[30] One of the things the Bible does really well is it gives a clear and unequivocal statement that men and women are of equal value in the sight of God. Still, their roles and functions are different, without elevating one's value above the other – what a balance!

ONENESS

It takes the average couple about nine to fourteen years for the two to stop thinking about themselves as "individuals" and to start thinking

---

[30] Richard L. Strauss, "2. They Shall Be One," Bible.org, accessed November 11, 2020, last modified June 28, 2004, https://bible.org/seriespage/2-they-shall-be-one.

about themselves as "one" – to go from "me" to "we." Thus, it should not be surprising that the average length of a marriage before it ends in divorce is eight years.[31] Going back to the Biblical text, verse 23 says, "And Adam said: 'This *is* now bone of my bones and flesh of my flesh; she shall be called Woman, because she was taken out of Man.'" By using the phrase "bone of my bones and flesh of my flesh," Adam was literally saying, "This one at last is bone my bones and flesh of my flesh!" Considering the activity he had just engaged in (i.e., naming all of the animals and their corresponding helpers), Adam may very well have emphasized the word **MY** in his statement above! After having named the animals and seeing each one with a corresponding companion, he was thrilled to see the "one" who corresponded to him. This helper, Eve, was literally formed from one of his bones! Even the Hebrew language provides a great illustration of this truth as the word "man" translates a Hebrew word **ISH**; whereas the word "woman" translates the Hebrew word **ISHAH**. This is what we would

---

[31] Curt Hamner, John Trent, Rebekah J. Byrd, Eric L. Johnson, and Erik Thoennes, Marriage: Its Foundation, Theology, and Mission in a Changing World, (Chicago: Moody Publishers, 2018), 112.

recognize as **positional** unity, as recognized by God once a couple is married.

Another observation is in order here. Notice Adam's full acceptance of the woman God created for him. Who did Adam know better at this point - God or the woman? He clearly knew God better at this point. Therefore, his acceptance of the woman was based solely upon his relationship with God. There was NO negotiation, NO complaints, and NO probationary period. There was immediate acceptance! Adam's full acceptance of God's good gift (i.e., Eve) was based solely on the fact that he trusted God's wisdom, **goodness**, and integrity. She was different, for sure, but Adam recognized that these differences must have been designed for his **good**. This is something we must realize in our own marriages - our mate's differences are good things God brings to us that He will use as tools to shape us into the people He wants us to be. Failure to accept and realize this often results in large levels of frustration. Not knowing completely how, why, when, and what. Adam accepted Eve as God's provision for his NEED. Eve was God's solution to it being "NOT GOOD."

INTIMACY

Verse 24 states, "Therefore, a man shall leave his father and mother and be joined to his wife, and they shall become one flesh." Now, this verse is probably an editorial comment by Moses more akin to saying, "This is **WHY** man leaves...," explaining the common practice of marriage in his day. Whereas ONENESS describes the positional unity that can never be changed and is an accomplished fact in the sight of God, INTIMACY reflects the **day-to-day** unity experienced by the couple as they remain in fellowship with one another. To "leave" means "to loosen, to relinquish/give up, or to forsake."[32] Now, in a marriage, this leaving could involve a physical leaving, an emotional leaving or detachment, or financial separation. Either way, this leaving is an actual transferring of dependence from one's parents to one's spouse. When this does not happen, and a pattern of going to parents for repeated assistance (financial, physical, emotional, etc.) develops, this can pose a serious threat to one's marriage. It may seem insignificant each time, but this is one of God's mechanisms to drive a couple to each other and to Him alone. Once the in-laws

---

[32] Swanson, DBL Hebrew, 6440.

consistently step in and meet the NEEDS of their married son or daughter, they undercut God's plan. Without "leaving," there can be NO cleaving! A quick command to in-laws: Lovingly '**shoo**' them back to their mates! Let the married couple learn how to meet one another's needs and to corporately trust the Lord for any other needs that may arise.

Now that we have considered "leaving," let's look more closely at the concept of "cleaving." To cleave means to cling to, to fasten oneself to, to be stuck together, and it conveys a strong emotional attachment.[33] Suffice it to say, this cannot happen unless one leaves, and one cannot truly leave unless they are clinging to someone else. These two concepts are **interdependent** upon one another. In fact, "cleaving" resembles weaving two threads into one new piece of cloth. No longer are two threads seen but only ONE where they have come together. It is this imagery that illustrates the phrase "become one flesh." Because there are conditions to be met by both husband and wife (i.e., leaving and cleaving), this one flesh description is definitely referring to the **day-to-day** unity of INTIMACY.

---

[33] Swanson, DBL Hebrew, 1815.

A Theology of Marriage

Thus, this reference is a physical reference to sexual intimacy and physical consummation (See Genesis 1:28). It is good to notice, too, that this level of ONENESS and INTIMACY is only said of a husband-wife relationship, not of a parent-child, a sibling-sibling, and a friend-friend, etc. Nothing, including the subsequent blessings of children, friends, and/or close family relationships should ever take priority over this God-ordained marriage relationship. This was something that God initiated and ordained within the bounds of marriage. Thus, sexual intimacy and unity in marriage is GOOD! There is a ONENESS created in marriage that God Himself has joined together (See Mark 10:9) and because God Himself has joined them together, there is no longer two but only one (See Mark 10:8). This truth is Paul's primary argument against sexual immorality in 1 Corinthians 6:12-20 - sexual intercourse CONNECTS you to the one you have sexual intercourse with and thus is designed to unite husband and wife in a way that no other relationship can.

TRANSPARENCY

According to a nationwide AARP survey, 75% of people admitted that they regularly lied to their significant other.[34] This is absolutely frightening and sickening to think about when we consider this last summary point of TRANSPARENCY. Verse 25 states, "And they were both naked, the man and his wife, and were not ashamed." Now, many do not attribute any significance at all to the fact that Adam and Eve were naked, but, because of the follow up phrase "and were not ashamed," it seems as if there is something the nakedness is to illustrate or symbolize. What is it? Because they were **BOTH** naked, they were both totally exposed to one another all the time. Nothing is ever being hidden or covered. Literally it means they were without "disguise or covering." Thus, they were without any fear of exploitation for evil. In this manner, they were totally vulnerable to one another, not holding anything back to protect themselves. They were totally TRANSPARENT to and with each other.

---

[34] Dr. Pepper Schwartz, "Is It Ever OK to Lie to Your Spouse?," AARP, accessed July 2, 2020, https://www.aarp.org/home-family/sex-intimacy/info-05-2012/pepper-schwartz-truth-about-lying.html#:~:text=If%20so%2C%20you're%20not,lie%20to%20a%20significant%20other.

This was in all the areas of intimacy, including sexual, emotional, and mental. Again, remember, this is especially reserved for a husband/wife relationship ONLY! There is no other relationship on earth with these types of privileges!

Joel Belz, writer for World Magazine, provides an apt conclusion for this chapter in his article entitled "That's What He Meant – Great Expectations: God Makes Terrific Marriages" when he says, "…I recall getting a strangely discomfiting message from other sources during my late adolescence. 'Marriage is OK,' I heard. 'But don't expect too much from it. It's hardly designed to put you in orbit.'…when I did marry and then discovered those flat spots every married person encounters, my instinctive response was to say, 'Oh, *this* is what they meant. *This* is why the veterans said, 'Don't expect overly much. It's OK – but don't expect heaven on earth.' So I didn't – and that was a poisonous concession…the problem with the lower 'realistic' standard is that pretty soon people buy into it. The lowered standard becomes what everyone starts shooting for – and then they start missing even that…I've determined to raise the standard high and to tell my children plainly: 'God made marriage good. No, that's not emphatic enough. He made marriage much better than good. He made it to be terrific.'"[35] May each one of us realize that God's design for marriage is terrific and may we refuse to settle for anything less!

---

[35] Joel Belz, "That's What He Meant – Great Expectations: God Makes Terrific Marriages," World Magazine, accessed January 6, 2021, last modified July 27, 2002, https://world.wng.org/2002/07/thats_what_he_meant.

CHAPTER 3
WHAT WENT WRONG?

The first step in most alcohol and/or drug addiction recovery is to **admit you have a problem**. In speaking of this first step in recovery from alcohol addiction, Alcoholics Anonymous puts it this way, "Who cares to admit complete defeat? Practically no one, of course. Every natural instinct cries out against the idea of personal powerlessness… No other kind of bankruptcy is like this one."[36] If a person thinks being drunk at 9 am is "normal" or if and individual thinks that stealing from his or her mother to buy drugs and living in a gutter is "normal," he or she will never admit there is a problem.

The United States leads the world in divorce. Puerto Rico is second, and Russia is third. To not admit, or to not recognize that America's culture has a problem when it comes to lasting marriage, is to not take the road towards a solution. However, more importantly, within the Church, having recognized God's original design for marriage, it is extremely valuable to

---

[36] Author Unknown, "Step One," Alcoholics Anonymous, accessed July 8, 2020, https://www.aa.org/assets/en_us/en_step1.pdf.

realize and admit that many marriages do not measure up to God's high standard. Each spouse in a marriage is needy, and it is NOT GOOD for the other to be alone. God made humankind needing: dependence, oneness, intimacy, and transparency. Again, the acronym is D.O.I.T. or "Do It!" So, if we know this, why can't we "just do it?" Is there something or someone working against God's plan?

Prussian Field Marshal Helmuth von Moltke the Elder made the statement, "No plan survives first contact with the enemy."[37] This is true of battle, which is the context in which Helmuth von Moltke made the statement, but it is also true of Biblical marriage. As one turns the page on the story in Genesis 2 of the first marriage and God's design for it, one sees something terrible develop in Genesis 3:1-7. Most of us know this story: Eve is deceived by a talking serpent, who tricks her into eating fruit from the one tree that God had instructed Adam not to eat from. Adam, in turn, passes along God's instructions to Eve, and so they should have been

---

[37] Author Unknown, "Helmuth von Moltke the Elder," Wikipedia, accessed July, 8, 2020, https://en.wikipedia.org/wiki/Helmuth_von_Moltke_the_Elder.

equipped to reject the serpent's temptation. However, they trust the serpent's words over and above God's Word, and they both eat of the fruit of the tree. This one act of disobedience totally re-directs people's lives on earth, and although God's plan for marriage did not change, individuals' ability to enjoy it and carry it out is severely altered and hindered. Humankind's fall allows sin to enter into the world with its natural consequences. Romans 5:12 states, "Therefore, just as through one man sin entered the world, and death through sin, and thus death spread to all men, because all sinned." Through one man (Adam), sin entered the world, and death came as a result of sin. Death permeated the entire human race, and remember - "death" in the Bible always refers to some kind of separation. Sin always produces death - **ALWAYS**! Now, "death" does not always refer to physical death, as it can refer to different types of deaths or separations. Physical death is the one we naturally think of, but there are others: (a) **Spiritual** – Separation between a person and God. When a person is born sinful, he or she is in this state of death; (b) **Relational** – Separation between two parties. An example of this is when a couple breaks up in their dating relationship and determines to no longer see each other; (c) **Dream**

– Separation between a person and a dream he or she had. An example of this is if that same couple who broke up were planning on getting married, their dream of marriage is no longer a possible reality, and thus that dream has died; (d) **Enjoyment of Life** – Separation between a person and his or her present enjoyment of life. An example of this is when a person sins and thus suffers the consequences of being out of fellowship with God and others. This could manifest in relationship difficulties, internal stress, internal anxiety, irritability, unthankfulness, bitterness, pent up anger, and so on. One thing is certain: death and separation will destroy the enjoyment of God's plan for marriage! In fact, death and separation are the very antitheses of what a marriage should be! In the verses following the Fall (Genesis 3:7-19), we get a closer look of what "death" looks like in marriage. It is the exact opposite of our acronym D.O.I.T. (Dependence, Oneness, Intimacy, and Transparency). Death in marriage will involve shame, guilt, loss of fellowship (both divine and with others), blame, and self-protection.

SHAME AND GUILT

Genesis 3:7-8 says, "Then the eyes of both of them were opened, and they knew that they *were* naked; and they sewed fig leaves together and made themselves coverings. And they heard the sound of the LORD God walking in the garden in the cool of the day, and Adam and his wife hid themselves from the presence of the LORD God among the trees of the garden." One of the incredible things about sin is its far-reaching effects. Sin not only ruins our relationship with God, but it also ruins and negatively alters our relationships with others. Ironically enough, sin also destroys one's theology. Look at how Adam, in the presence of the omnipresent Creator God, thinks that he can now hide from Him.

Immediately, one can see that shame enters the human race, and, whereas *transparency* was valued and designed for a healthy marriage, Adam and Eve now begin the process of *covering up*. Unfortunately, all their ancestors since then have also had this natural tendency. Before the Fall, covering up was unnatural, but now post-Fall, it is the default mode of one's sin nature. It is interesting to consider that something visible must have changed in Adam and Eve's appearance when they recognize their nakedness and feel the need to cover it (See Genesis 2:25). However, it begs the question, "**WHO** are they covering themselves up from?" There are only three people on earth at this time, so the answer is themselves, God, or themselves AND God. The latter seems to be clearly indicated based upon their desire to hide from God and cover themselves in the presence of one another. This is a problem and is not part of God's original design. This lack of **transparency** will ruin relationships in general, but it will specifically ruin ANY marriage that is lived in this way. Secrecy cannot exist in a healthy marriage. Many spouses will make a comment to each other such as, "That is none of your business!" These types of phrases should not be in a believing spouse's vocabulary! Nothing should be hidden from one's spouse. Yet, in the Church today, husbands and wives have different bank accounts, and they will not share password information on their phones, computers, or social media. Often married believers will have separate and hidden social media accounts from their spouses. Moreover, some spouses will not share what they did during the day - where they went or who they spoke to. Other spouses will never share what they are thinking, or what they are feeling. When all of these things are present, they are simply manifestations of the perversion of God's design for marriage. These things reveal a lack of value for what God values in a marriage - transparency with one another!

However, sin has even further reaching effects that just affecting one's horizontal marriage relationship. Sin also impacts one's vertical relationship or fellowship with God. In verse 8, Adam and Eve's shame also leads them to hide from God. Again *transparency* is de-valued as is *intimacy* with their Creator. The truly tragic thing about this is that they had known and loved God, and now they are hiding from Him. Again, sin always produces death (i.e., separation).

LOSS OF FELLOWSHIP

Additionally, verses 9-11 reveal a loss of fellowship with God. Verses 9-11 reads, "Then the LORD God called to Adam and said to him, "Where *are* you?" So he said, "I heard Your voice in the garden, and I was afraid because I was naked; and I hid myself." And He said, "Who told you that you *were* naked? Have you eaten from the tree of which I commanded you that you should not eat?" Sin ruined man's response to God, and it ruins mankind's response to his or her spouse.

Also, ironically, Adam does not answer God's question **directly**, nor does he offer up the real reason he was hiding. What Adam does do is he offers up a result of his disobedience (i.e., I was afraid because I was **naked**), rather than the true reason of disobedience (i.e., he ate of the fruit of the tree). Guilt, shame, and cover-up contribute to his ongoing lack of transparency with God. Adam should have come clean, and this was his opportunity to do so. Instead, Adam sins, attempts to cover up, and he avoids God, instead of running to Him. Adam specifically says he was "afraid" (of God), and we must remember that this was an entirely **new** emotion for Adam. He had never experienced or felt fear before, and, as a result, his natural reaction is to escape the consequences. One typically does that through a variety of excuses or self-justification, which leads us to another aspect of "death" in this story.

BLAME AND SELF-PROTECTION

Because of the fear experienced by Adam as a result of his sin, and his desire to escape the consequences of death, which unbeknownst to him had already started, Adam defends himself using the blame game. Verses 12-13 read, "Then the man said, 'The woman whom You gave *to be* with me, she gave me of the tree, and I ate.' And the LORD God said to the woman, 'What *is* this you have done?' The woman said, 'The serpent deceived me, and I ate.'" Fear sets in as Adam begins to contemplate the consequences for his actions, and immediately the *one-ness* and *dependency* God designed for marriage is negatively altered. Adam throws Eve "under the bus" and then backs over her a few times for good measure! At this very moment, Adam no longer *accepts* Eve as the spouse God gave to him. In fact, it is just the opposite - Adam blames Eve for the "mess" they are in. It is no longer "we," but now it is only "she." SHE could face the death penalty - SHE could suffer the consequences for both of us. For many husbands, they can relate to the same mentality that Adam had here. Every time a husband says, "Well, honey, if you didn't do XYZ, then I wouldn't have *yelled at you, used an angry tone, hit the wall, slammed down the milk* – You see, it was really all your fault, Dear."

However, just as Adam is responsible and accountable for his sin, so, too, is Eve. Eve, having been thrown under the bus, now blames the snake, and this situation quickly turns into a free-for-all. An "every man for himself" mentality takes over, and the *one-ness* and *dependency* that God designed for a healthy marriage are totally gone. Sin ruins everything because the consequence for sin is always death. And, lest we think that Adam and Eve are just a far off story that has nothing to do with our marriage, we again see the long-lasting and far-reaching results of sin.

ONGOING RESULTS OF SIN

Some ongoing results of the fall of man into sin are staggering, as it relates to marriage. Verses 16-19 read, "To the woman He said: 'I will greatly multiply your sorrow and your conception; in pain you shall bring forth children; your desire *shall be* for your husband, and he shall rule over you.' Then to Adam He said, 'Because you have heeded the voice of your wife, and have eaten from the tree of which I commanded you, saying, 'You shall not eat of it:' Cursed *is* the ground for your sake; in toil you shall eat *of* it all the days of your life. Both thorns and thistles it shall bring forth for you, and you shall eat the herb of the field. In the sweat of your face you shall eat bread till you return to the ground, for out of it you were taken; for dust you *are,* and to dust you shall return.'"

The first recorded result is for Eve AND all women in verse 16b - "Her desire shall be for her husband, and he will rule over her." The

What Went Wrong?

Hebrew word translated "desire" means to have a very strong emotion or feeling to have or do something.[38] Now, some might naturally think that this means that the woman will always have a strong desire to be with her husband. Unfortunately, this interpretation does not seem to work with either the context (we are in the middle of a verse pronouncing judgment on the woman) or the very next phrase… "and he shall rule over you," which seems to be set in contradistinction to it. In other words, it seems like "Her desire for her husband" is a negative thing, and that it is related to the next phrase, "He shall rule over you." The same word is used in Genesis 4:7, and it seems to help us in this regard because there the word is used as a strong desire to dominate. In Cain's case, the word is used of sin desiring to dominate him. So, putting this all together, what this phrase seems to be saying is that woman will possess a natural desire to dominate, influence, and/or control the marriage relationship with her husband. The NET Bible concurs by recording the verse this way: "You will want to

---

[38] James A. Swanson, <u>Dictionary of Biblical Languages with Semantic Domains : Hebrew (Old Testament)</u>, (Oak Harbor: Logos Research Systems, Inc., 1997), Electronic ed., 9592.

control your husband, but he will dominate you."[39] Thus, because of the Fall, sin has both corrupted the willing submission of the wife and the loving headship of the husband. Now, the husband no longer leads easily but must fight for his headship. Unfortunately, there is an inbred, "below the surface" battle always ready to rear its ugly head in the relationship. As a result, it is naturally difficult for the woman to place herself under her husband and his leadership, often times just naturally thinking she knows better, she can do better, she can do more efficiently, etc.

Now, and so the women do not feel like they are the only ones singled out, there are ongoing consequences making marriage difficult for the man as well. God tells Adam, "Because you have heeded the voice of your wife…" Wait a minute! I thought it was just because he ate of the tree? Well, apparently in eating from the tree at the suggestion of his wife, Adam yielded his God-ordained authority in the relationship to her as well. We learn later from the New Testament that although Eve was deceived, Adam

---

[39] Biblical Studies Press, LLC, *The NET Bible* (Richardson, TX: Biblical Studies Press, 1996).

was not, and he willingly and knowingly disobeyed God by taking the fruit of the tree.

Things have now changed for Adam too, and they will also have an impact upon his marriage relationship, along with every man who followed him. Whereas "work" was designed to be enjoyable and satisfying, now it would be difficult and would lead men to have to work harder to live. Work, too, would often be frustrating and difficult. Although this may sound like it would have little to no effect on one's marriage, this undoubtedly took some of man's focus and attention away from his wife and future family, causing self-sacrificial "love" for her to be naturally difficult. After all, he would have to work harder just to get things done to provide. Also, implied in this statement and the previous statement regarding women, is that men will have to "fight" and "battle" for their position as leaders. This type of battle causes some men to get bitter, upset, or feel threatened, and it causes other men to pull out the white flag of surrender, and they often retreat into their hobbies, friends, work, or other forms of perceived pleasure. They will go anywhere and do anything as long as they can get away from their wives. This is a huge mistake on the part of the husband, and as one writer says, "It is better to make a thousand little mistakes moving toward your wife than one big one retreating."[40] Again, this response and this attitude damages aspects (*oneness, transparency,* and *intimacy*) of God's original design for a healthy marriage.

So, as a quick summary statement regarding the ongoing results of the Fall on our marriages: making marriage work is going to be a battle! However, the battle is **NOT** against your spouse – it is NEVER against your spouse! Often times we get quickly worked up into a frenzy, believing that our spouse has changed sides and now is fighting for the enemy.[41] However, the truth of the matter is that my spouse and I are still ONE, and we will always remain ONE. Our enemy, on the other hand, is diabolical, maniacal, deceitful, persuasive, and deadly. Our enemy is organized in three coordinated entities known as the world, the flesh, and the devil (1 John

---

[40] J. Hampton Keathley IV, "Love Your Wife Sacrificially (Ephesians 5:25-27)," Bible.org, accessed July 8, 2020, last modified May 21, 2004, https://bible.org/article/love-your-wife-sacrificially-ephesians-525-27.

[41] "We no longer believe our spouse is for us, but instead has turned to be for another – we fear we will be hurt and exploited, and therefore instantly seek to protect ourselves." - Curt Hamner, John Trent, Rebekah J. Byrd, Eric L. Johnson, and Erik Thoennes, Marriage: Its Foundation, Theology, and Mission in a Changing World, (Chicago: Moody Publishers, 2018), 152.

2:14-17). These three coordinated entities are doing everything in their unrelenting power to work against God's design for your marriage. They are doing everything to work against God's best for you and your spouse – for your team!

One may ask, "So, what does it look like when the enemy is having his way in my marriage?" Well, Romans 7:15-25 is a great picture of what this will look like – abject failure and frustration. Whereas before you got married, you only had to deal with one sin nature (your own), once you get married, you are now dealing with two sin natures (yours and your spouse's). Remember, the sin nature or "indwelling sin," as Paul refers to it in Romans 7:17, is the very source of sin that every human being is born with at his or her physical birth. This "source" dominates every thought, word, and deed of the unbeliever, and, although the believer's relationship to sin has changed, this nature can also dominate the believer by default as he or she presents his or her body to it (See Romans 6:12-13). Needless to say, this is not a pretty sight based upon the works of the flesh, of living life from the source of sin, as recorded for us in Galatians 5:19-21a. When two people are joined together in marriage, their own sin natures make them completely self-focused and, hence, desirous to destroy the marriage. The natural thought process of a married person, walking according to the flesh, in one's marriage is: "I am fine," and "my spouse is the one who is messed up." Every thought will favor oneself when one is walking according to the flesh, making one less likely to accept responsibility and be accountable to his or her spouse, AND every thought will seek to blame one's spouse, even for the sinful way one is behaving. This is why walking according to the flesh is so dangerous and detrimental to marriage – this is truly what STINKS!

In this way, we must be convinced that our spouses are not "trying" to screw up, or "trying" to hurt us, or "trying" to be selfish. 2 Corinthians 5:15-17 is a very insightful passage which states, "And He died for all, that those who live should live no longer for themselves, but for Him who died for them and rose again. Therefore, from now on, we regard no one according to the flesh. Even though we have known Christ according to the flesh, yet now we know *Him thus* no longer. Therefore, if anyone *is* in Christ, *he is* a new creation; old things have passed away; behold, all things have become new." This passage tells us first that the life we live, we no longer live for ourselves. Our life is **NOT** about our comfort, getting our way, and having our dreams realized. This is true regardless if one is married or not. However, especially when we are married, this type of thinking should never be accepted as good or healthy. Additionally, we no longer view anyone, including our spouses, as someone in the flesh, but a miraculous "new creation" in Christ. Our whole perspective of our spouse can be a positive one, one in which we are amazed by looking at and living with an ongoing trophy of God's grace. As we take God's viewpoint on our spouse, and as we walk by means of the Spirit, the Spirit of God will produce **agape** love in and through you for your spouse! (1 Corinthians 13:4-7)

Ultimately, it is not hopeless to have a good and healthy marriage, but if you have no understanding of what is going on with your spouse, or what is going on with you, you have no hope of combating the problem properly. Again, the issues with you and the issues with your spouse are "normal" and "natural" and yet totally **NOT** acceptable, considering the divine resources at your disposal as a believer in Jesus Christ. Please do not feel or buy into the thinking that a mediocre or poor marriage is "as good as it gets!" Unfortunately, many of us have an addiction to a mediocre, or worse, a terrible marriage. We need to recognize there is a problem, an enemy, and that problem and enemy is **NOT** your spouse, contrary to the evidence that you may have laid out. You need your spouse to walk by means of the Spirit. However, and about one hundred times more important, your spouse **needs you** to "walk in the Spirit" (Galatians 5:16) and to respond to the Lord by faith in your moment-by-moment walk. In light of the resources you possess in Christ, you can withstand the onslaught of a carnal spouse and find your rest, peace, and joy in the Lord in the midst of anything. On the contrary, when you walk according to the flesh, or respond in a "tit for tat" manner with your carnal spouse, you can barely handle anything. Now that we know the problem, let's start working towards a solution!

CHAPTER 4
COMMON AREAS OF DISAGREEMENT

In the last chapter, it is clear how mankind's fall into sin and the subsequent lingering effects of that fall (i.e., man and woman's possession of an indwelling sin nature) have made the execution of God's original design for marriage very difficult. In fact, marriage is IMPOSSIBLE without the intervention and deliverance by God Himself. Now, this deliverance is not a deliverance from one's spouse, or from one's marriage, but rather each spouse's deliverance from his or her own sin nature.

As a review from the last chapter, man and woman both have a sin nature that desperately wants to destroy all of God's plan for marriage. Man and woman LOSE FELLOWSHIP with one another when they sin. Man and woman perpetrate SHAME and GUILT upon one another. Man and woman naturally BLAME the other person and go into SELF-PROTECTION mode. This removes the "we" concept of God's design for marriage, and it pits one another against each other, forming two "me's" in one relationship. Man and woman both have ONGOING RESULTS of the fall, especially as it relates to marriage. Now, men must FIGHT for their headship, and women naturally WANT the headship. Again, let's be real - marriage is a battle but NOT against one's spouse! God's ultimate goal for every individual is to focus on and attack the problem - NOT the person!

In this chapter, let's look at THREE areas that cause the most common disagreements between husbands and wives, and WHY our sin natures tend to gravitate towards these areas. Let's really **dig in our heels**! Obviously, this chapter will not be a comprehensive treatment of every problem that can arise in a marriage. However, by identifying the following three problems as the most common in the majority of marriages, my hope is that spouses begin to take a joint approach to recognizing and solving these problems.

COMMUNICATION

Ironically, the very first thing that needs to be discussed in the communication section has to do with communication. However, it has to do with us NOT moving our lips. It is called listening, and the age-old adage is true here - we have two ears and one mouth, so we can listen twice as much as we speak. One needs to understand that listening to your spouse has the ability to give perspective, information, and clues as to how, where, when you should respond. If you miss out on these, you are attempting to navigate relationships in the dark, and then you tend to REACT versus RESPOND! Imagine any dangerous activity performed in the dark (i.e., brain surgery, skydiving, driving with no lights, etc.) and know that communicating without first listening is on the same level and just as lethal!

In James 1:19-20, James gives three commands when he writes, "So then, my beloved brethren, let every man be (1st) swift to hear, (2nd) slow to speak, (3rd) slow to wrath; for the wrath of man does not produce the righteousness of God." Now, it is important to recognize a couple of important context clues in this passage. First, James has been talking about the proper way to respond to trials in one's life. The reason why believers can "count it all joy" (verse 2) when trials hit is because God has a positively designed outcome for trails – spiritual growth! So, when we come to these three commands, they are sandwiched in the context of receiving teaching as it relates to trials. The very first command has to do with listening. James says, "Let every man be swift to hear." The word "swift" means quick, swift, nimble; being ready, prompt.[42] The idea communicated is that we are to be **continually** hearing the Word of God and specifically listening to the encouragement to take divine viewpoint towards trials. This is something that we should readily and willingly be eager to receive.

The second command is "Let every man be slow to speak." The word "speak" means to talk at random; it is used especially of children with the meaning of talking too much, as in rambling on.[43] The idea communicated is to not rush out and say everything on one's mind, or everything one thinks he or she knows. Sometimes when one speaks, he or she insinuates that he or she "knows" something or has something of value to communicate when, in actuality, he or she does not. The individual should wait to obtain additional information and entertain the thought that "I may not be right, OR I may not have all of the information to communicate intelligently." This is much like children attempting to insert themselves into adult conversations. James is asserting here that it would

---

[42] Spiros Zodhiates, The Complete Word Study Dictionary: New Testament, (Chattanooga, TN: AMG Publishers, 1992), 5036.
[43] Zodhiates, The Complete Word Study Dictionary, 2980.

do his hearers good if they stopped talking, as it seems to prevent them from hearing the truth in a meaningful way.

The third and final command found in this passage is "Let every man be slow to wrath." The word "wrath" means anger as a state of mind; it is defined by Aristotle as **desire with grief**.[44] The word itself denotes a strong, persistent feeling of indignation and active anger. This type of anger is often a common result of disregarding the previous two commands: (1) not listening well enough to have the whole story, and (2) talking way too much when not having all the facts.

Another passage that builds on the concept of being a good listener is Proverbs 18:13, which states, "He who answers a matter before he hears *it,* it *is* folly and shame to him." The word translated by the phrase, "He who answers," means to bring back or return a comment.[45] The very fact that someone would bring back or return a comment to a matter or situation BEFORE he or she even hears it is described in two ways. First,

---

[44] Zodhiates, The Complete Word Study Dictionary, 3709.
[45] James A. Swanson, (1997). Dictionary of Biblical Languages with Semantic Domains : Hebrew (Old Testament), (Oak Harbor: Logos Research Systems, Inc., 1997), Electronic ed., 8740.

Solomon says, "It is folly," meaning that this approach in communication is foolishness and devoid of wisdom and understanding, oftentimes leading to evil.[46] So, when a person does not listen, he or she is even more susceptible to do evil! There is a pride involved in NOT listening – one is making an improper value assumption of the person to whom he or she is listening to. Often in marriages, this includes assuming and/or assigning improper motives to one's spouse.

Second, Solomon says this approach is, "Shame to him," meaning it is disgraceful, or humiliating; it communicates a painful, mental feeling.[47] This word was often used to describe someone of low status and thus reflects shame, low self-esteem, an internal feeling of failure and lack of worth. So, **WHY** does the sin nature dig its heels in here, as it relates to listening? Clearly, the sin nature produces selfishness in each one of us, thereby convincing us that the ONLY important thing that needs to be shared is what we have to say, AND everyone else should see it that way,

---

[46] Swanson, Dictionary of Biblical Languages, 222.
[47] Swanson, Dictionary of Biblical Languages, 4009.

too! This often shows itself in marital conflicts when one spouse is talking, and the other spouse is not really listening with an intent to understand but rather is thinking about what he or she is going to say next.

Now, that we have covered the most important part of communication —— listening, which involves not talking - what about when we do open our mouths in marriage? The first principles to consider are the principles of speaking the truth in love with sensitivity and respect. In other words, ask yourself are my words both truthful and loving with the aim of building up my mate in Christ? Do I take a genuine interest in my spouse — his or her dreams, feelings, likes or dislikes, and hopes? These questions encompass loving communication with interest, care, and respect.

Now, Ephesians 4:15 is often quoted here, "speaking the truth in love," but, if we look at the specific context, this verse is talking about sound doctrine. However, the principle of communication still applies, especially as we jump down in the chapter to verse 29, which reads, "Let no corrupt word proceed out of your mouth, but what is good for necessary edification, that it may impart grace to the hearers." Paul starts out with first describing how NOT to communicate. The word "corrupt" means to rot, and it was used of putrid, rotten vegetables, animals, or fruit on a tree.[48] Paul's point is emphatic — we are NOT to even allow these types of words to leave our mouths, touch our tongues, or burst through our lips. These types of words destroy and rot others! Often, in marriages, some spouses may say, "Well, it is the truth!" But, to **blast** your mate just because "that's just how you feel," may be truthful, but it is NOT loving. Also, and in contrast, to be dishonest about how you feel or not to say anything at all to avoid conflict may seem loving, but it is NOT truthful and will lead to long-term distance in the relationship. Hence, the principle of Ephesians 4:15 is applicable here – truthful speech spoken in love. Now, how or what does this look like?

In contrast to putrid and rotten words, one is to communicate good and healthy words, as the end of verse 29 states, "But what is good for necessary edification, that it may impart grace to the hearers." Notice that

---

[48] Zodhiates, The Complete Word Study Dictionary, 4550.

this type of "good" communication is described as "necessary"[49] to edify or build someone up. The contrast suggested is that "corrupt" communication will do the exact opposite of this – it will tear down! Many marriages engage in this type of destructive communication on a consistent basis. The very person with whom God has made us ONE with is the very person we seek to damage with our words, not realizing that it corrupts and putrefies us in the process.

However, notice the result of the "good" communication – this communication imparts grace (God's unmerited favor) to the hearers. Good communication to your spouse splashes them with grace! You might say, "Well, if you knew my spouse, you would know that he or she does not deserve it!" And, to that I say, "Amen!" That is the very definition of grace, and, while we are at it, can I let you in on a little secret? Your spouse has most likely said the same thing about you! What does your spouse need the most to grow spiritually and become more and more like the husband or

---

[49] Meaning a need or necessity – something you owe a debt to someone to do. Zodhiates, The Complete Word Study Dictionary, 5532.

wife that Jesus Christ wants he or she to be? The grace of God! (Titus 2:11-13) And, you can assist with that in the way that you rely upon the Lord in your communication with your spouse – splash your spouse, NOT **drown** him or her in Grace! Again, this is NOT just telling your spouse what he or she wants to hear and NEVER having a corrective word for your spouse. It IS paying close attention to the type of words you are using to communicate with him or her and even potentially your tone in doing so![50]

Now, this is great IF and only IF we can communicate like this consistently. But, when we do not do this well, there will be conflict. What then? One thing we must understand is that conflict in marriage is

---

[50] We all carry the consequences of others' sinful behavior toward us into marriage. Verbal or physical abuse by a parent, a former boyfriend/girlfriend, a stranger…the list goes on and on and can form the links of a strangling sinful chain to the past. In her irritated tone, we hear the voices of the past, belittling and demeaning us. In his playful sarcasm, we feel the sting of humiliation and de-valuation. Facing past wounds in marriage must be a two-way street. On one hand, the wounded partner must learn to trust his or her spouse, not holding them responsible for the sins of another while on the other hand, the opposite spouse must take these things into consideration and seek to be sensitive and more trustworthy in these areas. Without mutual trust and respect regarding past wounds, partners can easily find themselves tearing one another apart rather than building one another up. – Curt Hamner, John Trent, Rebekah J. Byrd, Eric L. Johnson, and Erik Thoennes, <u>Marriage: Its Foundation, Theology, and Mission in a Changing World</u>, (Chicago: Moody Publishers, 2018), 213.

inevitable[51], and married couples will invariably wrong one another. This unfortunately is a natural outcome of two human beings with indwelling sin living in close quarters. However, rather than recognizing this as a problem and putting our heads in the sand, it is very important to resolve conflict as soon as possible. In our marriages, we need to keep short accounts, as it relates to conflict, just like we are encouraged to do so in our fellowship with the Lord when we have sinned against Him. (1 John 1:9) For whatever reason, sweeping things under the rug has become a popular and yet ineffective way of dealing with conflict. This type of consistent approach to conflict resolution will create an ever-growing MONSTER of division in one's marriage.

As with the Lord in confession, taking personal responsibility and specific accountability for wrong actions, wrong attitudes, and wrong words are huge in true confession to our spouses. Biblical confession to the Lord

---

[51] Many couples avoid conflict like the plague, but we need to teach couples that the sign of a healthy marriage is not the absence of conflict, but how couples manage their conflict when it comes – as it will. Research consistently shows that one of the best predictors for marital success is when couples work through their problems in a healthy way. – Hamner, Marriage, 111.

or to our spouse is **NOT** "Yeah, I guess I'm a sinner," BUT specifically, "Here is HOW I have sinned against you, "OR" Here is WHAT I have done when I sinned against you."[52] "I have done this OR said this, and I was wrong." This is responsible accountability and clearly lets your spouse know that you recognize how you have harmed him or her. Now, the great thing about God is that He has promised forgiveness every time you confess your sins to Him. In fact, there is no need to ask for forgiveness from Him because the outcome is NEVER in doubt. 1 John 1:9 goes on to say that when we confess our sins, "He is faithful and just to forgive us our sins AND to cleanse us from all unrighteousness." God does not have an issue with forgiveness, and He is ready to immediately restore us to fellowship with Him. However, with our spouses, it is wise to ask for forgiveness while we confess our sins against them, owning specifically what we did wrong and calling it as it is![53]

---

[52] According to a biblical view of marriage, normal spouses who are relatively healthy bear responsibility before God and each other for how they treat each other, for their actions and inactions, and for the underlying state of their hearts toward their partner. – Hamner, Marriage, 111.
[53] If a husband loses his temper and yelled at his wife, he should not say, "I'm sorry that I yelled at you, but your whiny tone makes me angry!" He is blaming her for his sin. He

What we find from the Scriptures is that keeping short accounts of wrongdoing against our spouses is not just an optional approach, but it is necessary. In fact, there is great harm of not keeping short accounts of wrongdoings in relationships, especially in marriage. Hebrews 12:14-15 says, "Pursue peace with all *people,* and holiness, without which no one will see the Lord: looking carefully lest anyone fall short of the grace of God; lest any root of bitterness springing up cause trouble, and by this many become defiled." When the author uses the phrase translated, "looking carefully," it means to give attention to, or to look carefully, as if you were examining something.[54] In other words, this is something the author wants his readers to really dig into and pay close attention to. Also, continuing on

---

should not even say, "I'm sorry that I yelled at you," even though that may be true. In fact, she's probably sorry he yelled at her, too. Just saying that he is sorry DOES NOT indicate that he is taking personal responsibility for his sin. He is still NOT taking accountability before her for his personal wrongdoing. Many make this mistake in marriage by giving GENERAL acquiescence to having a problem. They say things like, "Well, yeah, I'm not perfect," or "Well, I am a sinner, I guess," or "Well, I'm sorry you had to marry someone who makes mistakes from time to time." The proper way to deal with personal sin is to say specifically, "God has convicted me of my sinful anger…I'm asking you, will you forgive me?" "When I said XYZ, I was wrong and very insensitive to your feelings…will you forgive me?" "When I told that joke about you in front of our friends, I had no idea that would embarrass you. I was wrong for doing that and I am sorry that I hurt you." Etc. Remember – Specific, Accountable, Responsible Confession!

[54] Zodhiates, The Complete Word Study Dictionary, 1983.

with the verse, it appears to say that if you and I do not pay close attention to pursuing peace with all people, we will "fall short of the grace of God." "Falling short" means to be last or to be behind. It means to miss out on or not take advantage of. In other words, grace resources are available if we will simply make a mental effort to pay attention to peaceful relations with our spouses and keep short accounts with them. It is important to recognize that our spouses need grace from us, and we must tap into God's grace to extend it to them – the resources are available! However, what if we DON'T? The verse goes on to say, "Lest any root of bitterness springing up cause trouble, and by this many become defiled." Notice, that bitterness springs up, grows over time, and causes trouble. "Causing trouble" means to disturb, to excite, or to annoy someone. In this case, it seems to refer to an internal disturbance and annoyance for the person who has refused to pursue peace with all people. This is where the damage sets in. Notice that bitterness does not stay isolated, but it spreads and stains others. It's like the flu – no one wants it, but it is extremely contagious!

A great illustration of unresolved conflict is given by Alicia Michelle, a contributor on Crosswalk.com, when she writes:

I think of unresolved tension in marriage like a pair of really dirty eyeglasses. Every time we have an argument or issue between us, our glasses (the lens of how we see each other) can get clouded and covered over with smudges, dirt and other debris. If we don't remove those "smudges" immediately through forgiveness and reconciliation, it becomes harder to see our spouses clearly (and it certainly becomes difficult to love and serve them unconditionally)! When these lenses are clouded, we don't want to forgive because it seems too difficult, too extreme. That one little issue we had last week has compounded with that other issue from today (plus that **reoccurring thing that drives us crazy!**) and before we know it, our hearts have shut down and our marriage is slowly dying. As hard as it seems, we must get to the root of our emotions and deal with these issues quickly with our spouses. We can't let things linger because of this compounding effect. **We must create the habit of dealing with these issues immediately and moving on** so that our marriages can operate freely and not be smothered by unresolved conflict.[55]

We must understand that the sin nature wants us to push conflict under the rug and NEVER deal with it because then there is a constant relational intimacy death that remains in place.

One final thing to consider in the area of communication is to not respond in kind if our spouses are walking in the flesh. Many times in our marriages, our spouses may be walking according to the flesh, and they may say something or use a certain tone that offends or upsets us. For many of us, this is when our gloves come off! We think, "If they are going to be that way to me, then I will respond in kind!" This is NEVER the right approach. In fact, we need to be reminded and encouraged and reminded again that NO ONE'S carnality towards us justifies our leaving fellowship with the Lord. Yet, this is often exactly what happens. Proverbs 15:1 says, "A soft answer turns away wrath, but a harsh word stirs up anger." A "soft answer"

---

[55] Alicia Michelle, "Five Signs Your Marriage is Headed for Trouble," Crosswalk.com, accessed July 10, 2020, https://www.crosswalk.com/family/marriage/5-signs-your-marriage-is-headed-for-trouble.html.

would be a Spirit-led answer, which has a healing effect on the situation because it turns away wrath. Now, this does not mean that you are to suspend truthful communication or give into whatever your spouse may be saying just because you desire to speak the truth in love. We may set up boundaries, clearly expressing our feelings, and communicate consequences. For instance, it may sound something like this, "You seem really upset right now. I want to hear what you are saying and would like to talk this through, but I do not think it would be good to do it right now. Let's pick this up later tonight."

Remember, in our marriages, we want to attack the problem, NOT the person. Often when your spouse is walking according to the flesh and behaving carnally, everything in you is going to want to self-protect, self-defend, and self-justify. Remember, from God's perspective, you and your spouse are on the same team – it may not appear that way at the time but recognize there is a problem, but IT IS NOT your spouse. The problem is two sin natures. Notice the second phrase in Proverbs 15:1, "A harsh word stirs up anger." The flesh always wants you to defend yourself because you are the #1 priority to your sin nature. Thus, you will fight, claw, bite, kick, and scream to respond in a similar manner, so your spouse feels the same way that he or she is making you feel. However, this type of response, governed by the sin nature, only produces more and more conflict and anger in the relationship. The flesh is getting exactly what it wants – destruction of your marriage relationship. Remember that ultimately God wants to be your Avenger (Romans 12:17-21), and God will judge righteously on your behalf (1 Peter 2:18-23). When you and I respond "in kind" to our spouses when they are walking in the flesh, we are defending ourselves and taking the spot God wants to take. Walking according to the flesh because your spouse is walking according to the flesh still HARMS YOU!

FINANCIAL MATTERS

The second of the THREE areas that cause the most common disagreements between husbands and wives is the area of financial matters. This, too, is another area that our sin natures tend to really **dig in its heels to**! We learn from a recent APA (American Psychological Association) that finances are the biggest cause of stress in the lives of 76% of Americans.[56] However, even more pertinent to the topic at hand, research amongst married couples have found that nearly 35% of people named money as the primary trouble spot with their partner...AND...financial problems are the leading cause of divorce.[57] Foolishly spending money, or the perception of foolish spending, is the number one financial cause for divorce. When a spouse **feels like** the other spends their money foolishly, it increases the likelihood of divorce by 45%. Researchers tell us that **perceptions** of how well one's spouse handles money play into those reactions.[58] It is the perceptions of one another that must be adjusted. One example illustrates this well: A woman who was married to an incredibly frugal man would go grocery shopping each week. When she got home, he would meticulously go through the newspaper, inspecting all the prices and coupons from other

---

[56] Nancy L. Anderson, "5 Financial Mistakes That Ruin Your Marriage," Forbes, accessed November 11, 2020, last modified November 10, 2011, https://www.forbes.com/sites/financialfinesse/2011/11/10/5-financial-mistakes-that-ruin-your-marriage-2/?sh=1112a47dafa5.

[57] Jessica Dickler, "Five Money Mistakes That Can Destroy a Marriage," CNBC, accessed November 11, 2020, last modified July 11, 2018, https://www.cnbc.com/2018/07/10/five-money-mistakes-that-can-destroy-a-marriage.html.

[58] Anderson, "5 Financial Mistakes That Ruin Your Marriage."

stores. He would then berate her if she could have gone to a different store and saved $0.50 on a block of cheese. He labeled this "foolish" spending, and he expected her to go to multiple stores (if needed) to save any money they could even though she worked full-time, and they had two children.[59] This may seem ridiculous to some, and yet to others this story may make a lot of sense! Hence, financial matters are crucial to understand, and it is beneficial to discuss the potential pitfalls.

One such pitfall is in the area of debt. There is much debate on the issue of debt within Christian circles and thus much difference of opinion. Some believers view any debt as legitimate and would take loans out on cars, education, boats, clothing, electronics, etc. Other believers think that some debt is okay, but only those loans that are taken out on an appreciating asset, such as a home mortgage. Yet, still others view all debt as wrong. It is because of this wide range of views on this topic that this is such a sensitive issue within marriages. Spouses do not always have the same view on this, and these things should be discussed before two people get married.

---

[59] Anderson, "5 Financial Mistakes That Ruin Your Marriage."

Also, typically, the building of debt is not the stressful part – it is the paying down of debt and agreement on the value of that and the rate at which the couple will pay it off. Some people bring their own debt into their marriage. Other couples incur additional debt during their marriage, either through individual spending or even joint agreement between the couple. Either way, the couple is now faced with debt and the prospect of paying off the debt, and this is where potential problems begin. As mentioned earlier, communication and having a plan are key! Once again, it is important to mention that you and your spouse are on the same team, that you are **WE** and not "he" or "she," and that debt is the problem, **NOT** your spouse! This is an area in which husbands and wives need to communicate their anxieties about having this debt OR communicate why they have **NO** anxieties about maintaining a certain level of debt. How can you listen to one another, respect one another, and work through these issues together? Much of the communication principles shared above will have direct application here, but there are also a couple of specific Biblical principles regarding money that need to be mentioned.

First, it is clear from the Scriptures that spending money one does not have is the very definition of coveting. The introduction of debt and credit into society tends to blur this line, but, if debt and credit did NOT exist, we would be able to recognize this more clearly in our own lives. Colossians 3:5 says, "Therefore put to death your members which are on the earth: fornication, uncleanness, passion, evil desire, and covetousness, **which is idolatry**." Paul identifies covetousness, meaning to desire something that you do not possess or something that is not yours, as idolatry. Ultimately, it is our hearts saying that we NEED something or someone else besides God, which makes an idol out of that thing. Whether we realize it or not, this is exactly what we are doing when we spend money that we do not have.

Second, it is important, both individually and as a couple, to learn to actively trust the Lord for the things you NEED **AND** for the things you WANT. Proverbs 3:5-6 applies here, "Trust in the LORD with all your heart, and lean not on your own understanding; In all your ways acknowledge Him, and He shall direct your paths." This is something that you and your partner need to agree would be beneficial for your marriage, and it would have the effect of putting you on the same team. Acknowledging God in all of your financial decisions and allowing Him to direct your paths has the effect of aligning both your interests. Between the two of you, develop a long and steady savings plan for these things and learn patience and self-control, which are things the Spirit of God wants to produce in you, as you walk in dependence upon the Lord. (Galatians 5:22-23)

Third, couples need to learn to prioritize and understand the difference between NEEDS and WANTS. Having an I-Phone is a WANT. Having food in the cupboard and refrigerator are NEEDS. Having steak and lobster in the freezer and all of your favorite chips and sports drinks in the cupboard is a WANT. Having the essentials of a well-balanced diet is a NEED. Having DirectTV or some form of satellite television with 500 channels is a WANT. Having electricity in your home, although one could manage without it, is closer to a NEED than a WANT. Getting your kids all the Christmas presents they want is a WANT. The list could go on and on. Couples need to sit down and get their expenses set out in front of them and decide together what is a WANT, and what is a NEED. Then, if you have a trusted friend, trusted relative, or trusted pastor, have them go over your own list and label what is a WANT and a NEED and see what they come up with that is different than yours.

As you deal with debt in your marriage, one of the things that couples must be aware of and take into account is the fact that each one of us possesses different money styles, and we must recognize and adjust to these differences in our spouse. Each spouse has his or her own money DNA, so to speak, and that is okay. However, to assume that one's spouse's DNA will be the same as his or her own leads to many disagreements and frustrations in marriage. Again, recognition of this and the ability to communicate through this will be key. To give an example, let us say that you and your spouse have an extra $300 at the end of a month. What will you do with it? The spouse that has the "spender" DNA might say, "Let us buy a new T.V.!" OR "Let's take the neighborhood out for ice cream!" The spouse with the "anxious" debtor DNA might say, "Let us put that as an extra payment on one of our debt bills!" The spouse with a "saver" DNA might say, "Let us put that in our long-term savings because we never know when we might have a rainy day!" A spouse with a "retirement planner"

DNA might say, "Let us put that in our 401K!" These four types of DNA already give us a picture of what could be a massive problem! Once again, any crack in the marriage relationship that can be used by the sin nature of one or both spouses WILL BE used to try to cause more division!

Another financial pitfall that can arise within a marriage involves one's family. In the immediate family, how important will it be to you and your spouse for your children to be able to do all of the activities they want to do. At what point are music lessons and recitals, horseback riding lessons, gymnastics, other traveling sports, or academic camps enough? Some parents, due to their love for their children, never think "enough is enough." They will beg, borrow, and steal (figuratively speaking) to make sure their children can be a part of anything they want to be a part of. However, some parents, also due to their love for their children, realize that the family's world does not revolve around one child, and that, in the long run, that type of single-hearted devotion might harm the child. Even apart from the intrapersonal relationships and the impact on those, what about the gobs of money going out the window to support this child or these children? If there are differences of opinion and differences of spending

DNA between the couple, there remains a chance for incredible fireworks. Again, sensing a crack, the sin nature will dive in to try to make a huge divide between spouses over the aforementioned scenarios.

Another potential family pitfall involves married couples' relatives who need financial assistance. For instance, what does one spouse do when one of his or her siblings needs financial assistance? What does the other spouse do when one or both of his or her parents needs a rent payment? What do spouses do when one of their grown children needs help? These are very real scenarios that happen all the time, and they cause great damage in marital relationships. One spouse feels obligated to help and feels like it would be sinful or selfish NOT to help, while the other spouse feels zero obligation and feels like helping would be a waste of money and potentially a waste of investment on someone who is not responsible. One spouse wants to love with open hands, and the other spouse wants to love with more of a tough love. These are very real situations that can cause some very serious ONENESS problems within marriage.

Speaking of ONENESS, another major problem that can develop in the area of finances is deceit. It is estimated that in at least two out of

Common Areas of Disagreement 73

five couples, one spouse admits to having lied to his or her partner about money.[60] For many people, rather than dealing with the potential conflicts raised by different money styles or different opinions on spending, spouses often hide and deceive their partners about their spending or saving. This is financial infidelity and can break trust within a marriage, just as much as sexual infidelity can. To hide debt before or after marriage from one's spouse is deceitful and should never be considered. Moreover, to hide additional savings from one's spouse is deceitful and should never even be considered. Be assured that if you feel you have to hide something, regarding finances from your spouse, that type of thinking is coming from the FLESH. 1 Peter 2:1 says, "Therefore, laying aside all malice, **all deceit**, hypocrisy, envy, and all evil speaking." Please understand that if you cannot trust your spouse with finances or if he or she feels like they cannot trust you, then you need to have more conversations. You need to learn how to communicate with and adjust to one another. Unfortunately, many spouses take a more dangerous, yet expedient view wherein they give up on their

---

[60] Dickler, "Five Money Mistakes That Can Destroy a Marriage."

spouses, and they start setting themselves up as independent entities. This flies right in the face of one of God's design for your marriage – ONENESS! Combining incomes, bank accounts, and tackling debt, bills, and purchases together can have a natural "connection" factor for a marriage. Although these things may produce more conflict, remember conflict is NOT unhealthy; rather, it is one's response to conflicts that can be. Conflict requires some effort, but, in the long run, it is worth it if it has the ability to bring more ONENESS within a marriage.

The last of the THREE areas that causes the most common disagreements between husbands and wives is the area of child-rearing. Statistics show that disagreements about child-rearing is a growing reason for divorce.[61] The amount of areas that couples can disagree on in the area of child-rearing is almost too numerous to list. Should the baby sleep in our bed? If so, for how long? Should we use breastmilk, formula, or a combination of the two? How should we school our kids? What type of

---

[61] Focus on the Family, "Potential Child-Rearing Conflicts Between New Parents," accessed November 11, 2020, last modified 2006, https://www.focusonthefamily.com/family-qa/potential-child-rearing-conflicts-between-new-parents/.

activities should we allow our kids to engage in, and in what frequency? What about discipline? Will we spank, give time outs, or just give lectures? Do we do a combination of all three? If so, what constitutes a spanking versus just a time out? What age does the discipline change, if ever? Maybe the couple agrees on discipline style, but what if one parent is too strict, and one is too soft? Moreover, what if one spouse is consistent, and the other spouse is inconsistent? Is one spouse overprotective, while the other is not protective enough? Will you disagree and/or argue in front of the kids? If so, what will be acceptable, and what is too private of a topic to discuss in front of the kids? Should we be saving for college, or should we be spending money on the children and their activities now? How should we select a church? Should we select a church based on the child's perceived needs (i.e., a youth group, friends for them, a lot of programs, and good activities) or based on other items (i.e., doctrine and music)? What does your older child need – more empathy, more of a pat-on-the-back, or a kick in the butt? How much guidance/advice should you give in areas of life's decisions – college, religion/beliefs, career, or a future spouse? These questions and many more infiltrate one's marriage at a rapid-fire pace.

Clearly, children are people whose lives married couples feel very passionate about, and thus when couples are NOT on the same page, passionate disagreement can lead to huge conflicts. These conflicts have the potential to lead to huge blow-ups within a marriage relationship. Sometimes, being aware of the problems, can help us be on guard in these areas and begin to recognize and realize the need for a solution – a solution that only comes from outside ourselves — a solution that can only come from the Lord. So, what is OR are the solution(s) to these and other problems that arise in marriage?

The Solution – GOD'S PART — You must be filled "by the Spirit"

Being filled by the Spirit is the key to all the instruction on marriage found in Ephesians 5. Ephesians 5:18 precedes both Ephesians 5:22 and Ephesians 5:25. To be filled "by the Spirit" means that the Spirit of God is the filling agent, and He is filling the believer with the life of Jesus Christ. Galatians 2:20 says it this way: "I have been crucified with Christ; **it is no longer I who live, but Christ lives in me; and the life which I now live in the flesh I live by faith in the Son of God**, who loved me and gave Himself for me." The Spirit of God, and He alone, possesses the power to free believers from the power of sin. Just as humankind needs a Savior to deliver them from the penalty of sin, so, too, believers need a Savior to deliver them from the power of sin in their daily lives. Circumstances should never in and of themselves dictate to a believer whether or not he or she is in fellowship with the Lord. When not in fellowship with the Lord, the believer is 100% dominated by the sin nature. It is only the Spirit of God who can deliver the believer from this bondage.

When we consider the main areas of disagreement above, many of these situations are not "cut and dry" OR "black and white" issues. Hence, handling not only the situations with wisdom, but also dealing with one's spouse in wisdom, understanding, and grace are keys to a Christ-honoring marriage. Again, a person can have all the right desires in the world, but the ability to execute those desires lies solely at the feet of the Holy Spirit. Paul found this out the hard way, as he describes his experience in Romans 7:14-25. In this passage, the personal pronouns "I," "me," "my" are used over 40 times, whereas the Holy Spirit is mentioned zero times. The result? The things Paul wanted to do, he could not do, and the things Paul wanted to stop doing, he could not stop. It is not until Romans 7:24 that Paul asks the right question: it is NOT "what will deliver me?" but rather "WHO will deliver me?" Romans 7:25 provides the answer – it is the life of Jesus Christ produced in the life of the believer via the indwelling Holy Spirit.

The Solution – MAN'S PART — You must walk by faith

The problem with many of us is that we like to "walk by sight" and see everything all the way through to the end. We like to quote Proverbs 3:5-6 which states, "Trust in the LORD with all your heart, and lean not on your own understanding; In all your ways acknowledge Him, and He shall direct your paths." However, in all reality, we live a much different reality. Our reality is "DO NOT trust in the Lord at all and lean HEAVILY on our own understanding; NEVER acknowledge the Lord in anything we do, and we CAN direct our own paths." Many times a decision must be made, in a thousand daily moments, to trust God's word and His principles and not try to self-protect. Unfortunately, for many of us, the temptation is too great, and our reaction to circumstances and our spouses is to not respond to the Lord by faith. In the area of finances, we begin hiding money in a separate bank account, because our spouses spend too much of it, instead of continuing to speak to our spouses, holding them accountable by

Common Areas of Disagreement 79

confronting them on their bad habits. Our attitude should be one of trusting the Lord and praying for our spouses, remaining patient as the Spirit of God produces patience within us (Galatians 5:22).

At all times, but especially in these times of difficulty and disagreement, husbands and wives need to live in a vacuum with Jesus Christ. Both need to learn how to RESPOND to the Lord and NOT to REACT to their spouses. We all have a tendency to read our spouse's "mail" to the detriment of reading our own. In fact, it can be safely said that many men probably know Ephesians 5:22 better than 5:25, and many wives know Ephesians 5:25 better than 5:22. Just remember — your spouse's carnality, in any of these areas, is NEVER an excuse for a carnal RESPONSE from you! Walking by faith and relying upon God's resources, specifically what He did to free you from sin's power via your co-crucifixion and co-resurrection with Jesus Christ (Romans 6:1-14), is your only chance to navigate these areas of disagreement with your spouse and to suffer the least amount of damage to your relationship

CHAPTER 5
SPOUSE HUNTING PART 1

The last two chapters may have sounded familiar and, at times, unpleasant to those who are married. They may have even been downright scary for those who are not yet married! Even the best of marriages experience times and seasons of intense conflict and disagreement. So, if that is the case, what should those do who have yet to be married? Should they just throw in the towel and have the attitude, "Well, it is going to be horrible anyway, so it does not really matter who I marry!" Moreover, should they just never get married? As with everything in life, these questions must be asked in consideration of the Lord and His will for each individual. In fact, the first question single believers should ask is not **WHEN** or **HOW** they will get married, but **SHOULD** they get married at all?

In Paul's first epistle to the church at Corinth, he addresses these aforementioned issues. The context of chapter 7 involves Paul's response to a specific question from the Corinthian church as evidenced by verse 1: "Now concerning the things of which you wrote to me…" Additionally, we gather from verse 26 that there are some sort of distressing circumstances that were presently going on in Corinth. Verse 26 reads, "I supposed that this is good because of the present distress – that it is good for a man to remain as he is." What is the present distress or crisis to which the Apostle refers? It may have been a crisis in the Corinthian church or in Corinth in which there is no more specific information. However, in view of Paul's description of this distress found in verses 29–31, it seems as though he is speaking about the fact that the Corinthians were living in the "last days." If this is correct, we, too, live in the same **present distress** as the Corinthian believers did.[62] Therefore, the advice that the Apostle Paul gives in chapter 7 - in response to a direct question from the Corinthians believers (**peri de**) - applies to believers today.

In verse 7, Paul says, "For I wish that all men were even as I myself. But each one has his own gift from God, one in this manner and another in that." The word Paul uses here translated "wish" means to will, to wish,

---

[62] Tom Constable, "Notes on 1 Corinthians," *Plano Bible Chapel*, last modified 2020, accessed August 23, 2020, https://www.planobiblechapel.org/tcon/notes/html/nt/1corinthians/1corinthians.htm.

to desire.[63] It implies active volition and purpose. Paul is simply stating that if he got his wish, he would want all single Christian people to remain single. Now he has his reason for this, which we will look at later in verses 32-35, but, for now, it is important to note what his general preference is.

However, Paul recognizes that it is not about his own general preference, nor is it about forcing his own personal preference on other people. The next phrase in verse 7 says in contrast, "But each one has his own gift from God, one in this manner and another in that." So, even though Paul has a certain way he would personally like to see things work, he also recognizes that God may have other plans for each individual believer. By implication and context, Paul mentions two gifts here: (1) The married life, and (2) The single life. Notice that both gifts have the SAME source. Each one of these giftings come from God. Now, we know that God knows exactly what He is doing and the best kind of gifting for each one of His children. Since this is true, can we see that being married or

---

[63] Spiros Zodhiates, The Complete Word Study Dictionary: New Testament, (Chattanooga, TN: AMG Publishers, 1992), 2309.

single has no bearing or impact on one's value to the Lord and, by implication, no negative bearing on the local church?! God sees value and intrinsic worth in every believer, regardless of one's marital status because of one's unchanging position IN Jesus Christ!

So, this is very helpful to know if one is a single believer "spouse hunting." As believers, we should not hold up marriage as the "end all, be all" for every Christian youth, college, or career age person in our church body. It literally may not be for all of them! Getting married could literally take some of them out of God's gifting in their lives. In fact, God may have specifically designed singleness for certain individual believers. So, that begs the question: "How does one know which one they are, or which gifting they have received?" Paul tries to help with this question in verses 8-9 when he states, "But I say to the unmarried and to the widows: it is good for them if they remain even as I am, but if they cannot exercise self-control, let them marry. For it is better to marry than to burn with passion." Again, Paul expresses his wish for single believers to remain single, but he gives a caveat to his personal desire – that caveat is: "But if they cannot exercise self-control, let them marry." The phrase translated "exercise self-control" translates one Greek word meaning to be temperate or to have complete control over one's emotions, desires and actions.[64] As the text further reveals, Paul is clearly talking about self-control in the area of sexual intimacy, as he describes in the next phrase – "It is better to marry to satisfy that desire than to burn with passion." It is also interesting to note the word Paul uses to negate this phrase – the word translated "cannot" is a full and objective negation, independent of other circumstances.[65] Thus, the significance of this word choice is not necessarily one of the following: (1) They cannot maintain "self-control" because they are animals, or (2) They live in a corrupt culture like Corinth, or (3) This is "just what young men and young women do, so they cannot help themselves!" What Paul seems to imply by this word choice is that due to God's gifting of singleness or marriage, some believers are wired for marriage and the sexual benefits and blessings that come from that relationship. So, if that is the case, they should pursue marriage and not remain single. To try to take a believer who

---

[64] Zodhiates, The Complete Word Study New Testament, 1467.
[65] Zodhiates, The Complete Word Study New Testament, 3756.

has been "gifted" marriage by the Lord and force him or her to be single would put him or her in a real predicament and temptation to sin.

In contrast, why is Paul's desire that single believers stay single? It is a very simple reason; Paul wants single believers to be able to serve the Lord with the least amount of earthly distractions. There are jobs, ministries, and callings that suit single people better than someone who is married or even married with children. These jobs must be done to build Jesus Christ's church, but they are more difficult for married people to perform. Paul says it this way in verse 35, "And this I say for your own profit, not that I may put a leash on you, but for what is proper, and that you may serve the Lord without distraction." When Paul says "serve the Lord," he uses a unique word used only here in the New Testament, (**euprosedros**) meaning to sit close by, giving the idea of a constant attendant, and to give continual devotion as a servant.[66] The idea communicated is that this person would be supremely available to the Lord for whatever, whenever, and however the Lord needed them. We know this

---

[66] Zodhiates, The Complete Word Study New Testament, 2145.

because of how Paul goes on to clarify the phrase "serving the Lord" with the phrase "without distraction." What would distract from this type of unfettered attention and devotion to the Lord? The context tells us that our spouses **ARE** this distraction in verses 33-34. By the way, this is okay and not sinful for those "gifted" with marriage. God has a ministry for married individual believers, not *ONLY* to others, but also to their spouses and any future potential family members produced from that union. However, distraction would not be okay for those "gifted" with singleness, as God has other plans in mind for them.

GENERIC DO'S IN SPOUSE HUNTING

First, and foremost, the person you are looking for must be a believer. This would seem to be naturally and universally agreed upon, but you may be surprised. Unbelievers should NOT be pursued for a marriage relationship. 2 Corinthians 6:14 says, "Do not be unequally yoked together with unbelievers. For what fellowship has righteousness with lawlessness? And what communion has light with darkness?" Marriage is a joining together of two people into ONE. God's design is NOT to yoke up a believer (who is light) with an unbeliever (who is darkness) in a ONE

FLESH relationship. Now, in this world, you are going to work with unbelievers, go to school with unbelievers, be neighbors with unbelievers, and even go to church with unbelievers; but the ONE FLESH relationship of marriage is sacred and designed to function a certain way. This principle is never to be violated, regardless of "how good he looks in a pair of jeans" or "how pretty her smile is."

In fact, think of it this way: would you ever knowingly sign up for severe pain; severe heartache, or overwhelming frustration and hurt? Most sane people would answer quickly and firmly with "NO!" However, have you ever considered the fact that if a believer knowingly makes the decision to marry an unbeliever, he or she is signing up for just this type of life? An unbeliever only has one SOURCE from which to live his or her life – the sin nature, the flesh, or the indwelling power of sin. This means that 100% of the time this person is governed by his or her selfish sin-nature and, even in their most pleasant moments, his or her actions, attitudes, and words are all tainted, whether consciously or subconsciously, by impure motives. In fact, that is just the "acceptable" (to us) side of the sin nature – the side that is NOT blatantly or overtly harmful. But, what about Galatians 5:19-21, which says, "Now the works of the flesh are evident, which are: adultery, fornication, uncleanness, lewdness, idolatry, sorcery, hatred, contentions, jealousies, outbursts of wrath, selfish ambitions, dissensions, heresies, envy, murders, drunkenness, revelries, and the like; of which I tell you beforehand, just as I also told *you* in time past, that those who practice such things will not inherit the kingdom of God." What sane person would sign up for that? Yet, sadly enough, every believer who chooses to buck the wisdom of the Word of God is signing up for this, as this is what the sin nature produces. Again, it may not show up right away, and it may not reveal itself very often, but it is there, always lurking because this is the **ONLY** *SOURCE* from which an unbeliever can live his or her life.

Therefore, having addressed the first and most primary knock-out factor, whether or not he or she is saved, what are some other things to look for as a believer "spouse hunts" for another believer. The first question has to be: "Is he or she pursuing the Lord?" Proverbs 1:7 and Proverbs 31:30 both emphasize the value of "fearing the Lord." Proverbs 1:7 says, "The fear of the LORD *is* the beginning of knowledge, *but* fools despise wisdom and instruction," and Proverbs 31:30 says, "Charm *is* deceitful and beauty *is* passing, but a woman *who* fears the LORD, she shall be praised." To "fear the Lord" means to show such reverence, respect, and awe of the Lord that one considers Him in everything one does, says, or thinks. Everything in one's life runs through the grid of the Divine Viewpoint – how would God think, feel, respond about this thought, word, or action? This type of person is going to place a high value on what the Lord places a high value on. This type of person is going to desire to prioritize things in life the way the Lord prioritizes things in life. Now, although this next statement should be readily understood, it must still be stated: just because someone tells you he or she is pursuing the Lord, it does not necessarily mean that he or she is pursuing the Lord. Anyone will say that if he or she thinks that he or she can connect with you, and that person will tell you what he or she thinks you want to hear. So, "spouse hunting" believers must be careful and wise, and they must be on the lookout for certain things. Now, potential spouses are NOT going to be perfect. That is NOT the point, NOR is that the target you are looking for when "spouse hunting." However, you can observe potential habits, patterns, or values by paying attention to some very specific things.

Although not a foolproof or comprehensive list, here are ten suggestions regarding some very specific areas:

1. Does the person respond and change his or her mind when confronted by the Word of God? Nobody is going to be perfectly doctrinally sound, nor is anybody going to respond perfectly to every difficult situation in life. This is NOT talking about perfection. This is talking about someone who when confronted by something in the Word of God that is different from what he or she has previously thought or what he or she has always thought, takes careful study and consideration, and changes his or her mind to align with the Word of God. This is HUGE! If a person cannot or will not respond to the authority of God's Word in his or her life, you need to RUN! This is an indicator that he or she is NOT truly pursuing the Lord. It is NOT to say that he or she will never pursue the Lord, but it is to say you do NOT want to "roll the dice" on this type of person in a marriage relationship. If he or she will NOT yield to the authority of the Word of God he or she is carnally-minded and proud.

2. Does the person listen to the instruction of his or her parents? Immediately, I can hear some saying, "Why does this matter? Who cares how they respond to their parents? We are not going to be living with their parents!" Here's why it matters: your potential spouse's parents are an established and clearly defined authority structure in life. God has placed this authority structure in place, and, if the potential spouse is comfortable ram-rodding, ignoring, or de-valuing God's established authority structure here, then he or she will potentially be much more comfortable doing the same thing with other clearly defined precepts in the Word of God. If the person is not willing to listen to, consider, respect, and value his or her parents' instruction, that person is, in essence, training him or herself to be a rebel. This is NOT the type of spouse you want. You do not want a spouse who, does not like what his or her boss said to them, and so they are going to give them a "piece of their mind," and get fired over it! You do not want a spouse who determines that he or she is going to rebel against the government in some way (taxes, fees, requests, etc.) and suffers the consequences. You do

not want a spouse who determines that the church leaders are "a bunch of idiots" then stirs up trouble. In other words, this type of person is training his or herself to be the type of person who constantly "bucks against" every type of authority in life. Proverbs 1:8-9 says, "My son, hear the instruction of your father, and do not forsake the law of your mother; For they *will be* a graceful ornament on your head, and chains about your neck." On the flip side, if a person listens to the instruction of his or her parents and values their position in his or her life, he or she will have ongoing benefits, as communicated by the phrases "a graceful ornament on your head" and "chains about your neck." In other words, that person's life and character will be adorned by the benefits of positively responding to his or her parents.

3. Does the person value and seek to obtain wise counsel in his or her decisions? Although, at times, it seems nice to be with someone who is decisive, please recognize that if you are single and spouse hunting, you need to find somebody who realizes that he or she does not know everything. As simple as that sounds, please take

this to heart! The truth of the matter is that the person you are interested in DOES NOT KNOW everything! However, does he or she realize it? Proverbs 1:5 says, "A wise *man* will hear and increase learning, and a man of understanding will attain wise counsel." Proverbs 12:15 says, "The way of a fool *is* right in his own eyes, but he who heeds counsel *is* wise." If the person is able to recognize that they potentially do not know something, and as a result that they should not jump to conclusions, they are on the right track. If the person can recognize that maybe they should not confront someone just now because maybe they do not have all of the facts, or maybe they DO NOT know someone's motives, or that maybe they should approach this situation with grace and humility instead of a pickax and blowtorch, then they are on the right track. However a person approaches these things before you are married is most likely the way he or she is going to approach these things when you are married. The same treatment the person is giving others (i.e., assuming the worst in their motives, making bold confrontations without all of the facts, etc.) is going to be the same way the person treats you.

4. Who are the person's friends? What are they like? Is the individual a "good" friend to others? If a potential spouse tells you, "Oh, I am pursing the Lord Jesus Christ, and I am walking with the Lord," and then they have a group of friends that are into questionable and/or sinful activities, that is a potential red flag. Generally, people who are into sinful lifestyles do not like to hang around people that are into spiritual things. That is just the nature of how it works – these two types of groups generally do not attract one another (Proverbs 1:10-19). Maybe the person's friends are not "outwardly" sinful, but you can tell that they are NOT really into spiritual things either. Having hung around them, you can tell that his or her friends are apathetic towards spiritual things and very secular/carnal in the way they approach life. Again, there is nothing "outwardly" sinful but just a general worldly focus with worldly aims in life. These types of things could be an indicator that your potential spouse is not as interested in spiritual things as he or she claims. Additionally,

another area of observation is in the area of how your potential spouse treats his or her friends. Proverbs 17:17 says, "A friend loves at all times, and a brother is born for adversity." You can learn a lot about somebody by the way he or she treats his or her friends. Does the person abandon them when times get tough? Does her or she put on a big smile and say, "Oh, I just love your new shoes!" and then go over in the corner and criticize his or her ugly shoes to a different group of friends? Is he or she willing to blow off commitments to his or her friends if something else comes up that he or she is more interested in? Does the person ignore his or her friends when they call or text? How does he or she handle conflict with his or her friends? Does the person give them the silent treatment? Does her or she have a history of damaged and destroyed relationships in the past? All these things will one day transfer to your potential marriage because the works of the flesh do not just "pump their brakes" when you get married. The same sin nature will be present then as it is for your future spouse now, and, if he or she is not walking by means of the Spirit, who can deliver you from this type of mistreatment from the potential spouse as well?

5. Does the person gossip? If you can tell that a potential spouse loves to soak up and soak in every amount of information from someone else, and you witness him or her sharing it all with someone else, this is a major problem. Some people LIVE for the sordid, juicy morsels of information about other people, so they can share it. Many people who struggle with gossip have perfected the art of sharing information in such a way that they appear NOT to be gossiping. They are clever in how they bring information up, how they drop it into a conversation, or how they feign concern and ask for prayer for "so and so." Just know this, that if your potential future spouse is a gossip about others, he or she will one day gossip about you. She will be the wife that is down at the coffee shop with five friends talking about how you are an awful husband, how you screw up everything you do, how your attitude is awful, how you do not treat the kids right, how you kick the dog, and how everything you do and every one of your faults is ruining your life

and your kids' lives. Or, this will be the husband at the office coffee pot, griping about how his wife is always "on him," how she does not appreciate all that he does by providing for the family, how she overreacts to everything going on in their lives, how she overspends on things she does not really need, how she babies the children, how she is never interested in physical intimacy, and how she is crazy and ruining his life. A couple of verses from Proverbs summarize the strife and pain gossips stir up and show the necessary response to someone who is a gossip. Proverbs 26:20 says, "Where *there is* no wood, the fire goes out; and where *there is* no talebearer, strife ceases." Proverbs 20:19 says, "He who goes about *as* a talebearer reveals secrets; therefore do not associate with one who flatters with his lips."

6. How well does the person take correction? Does he or she at least see the value in correction? I love it when the Bible is raw, real, and brutally honest. Proverbs 12:1 is one such verse, as it addresses the concept of receiving correction. It states, "Whoever loves instruction loves knowledge, but he who hates correction *is* stupid."

Wow! Can it get any more raw or real than that? Now, how many of us really take correction well? Maybe, even as you consider your own response to correction, you realize this is an area you can grow in. Correction is NOT comfortable or enjoyable for any of us. However, do you recognize and realize that it is GOOD for you? Are you committed to that concept? Are you bought in enough to recognize and see the high value that correction can place in your Christian life and in your spiritual growth? Some people get angry initially with the messenger and/or the message of correction, and then later, when they are thinking biblically, they realize, "You know what! I appreciate what that person said to me because I know that he or she actually loves me. This is really going to benefit my spiritual life going forward." However, when someone does not value correction, he or she typically views the person who corrected him or her as public enemy number one for the rest of his or her life. People who do not value correction often have a long list of people that they have completely "written off" over the course of their lives. Again, because humility must be present in order to receive correction, a lack of value for correction indicates someone who is being dominated by the sin nature. This person is NOT spiritually-minded and is someone who does NOT realize how desperately he or she needs to be in fellowship with the Lord.

7. How does the person handle trials? Do her or she have a biblical perspective on trials? James 1:2-4 provides a biblical understanding and response to trials (albeit a supernatural one) when it states, "My brethren, count it all joy when you fall into various trials, knowing that the testing of your faith produces patience. But let patience have *its* perfect work, that you may be perfect and complete, lacking nothing." You know it is a one thing for a person to talk about "counting it all joy," concerning trials, at a Bible study on Sunday morning or at your devotional study time on Tuesday early morning, but what about when a trial hits him or her on Wednesday afternoon? What is his or her response? Does the person immediately begin to devise self-reliant strategies of mitigating the negative circumstances or does he or she end up in a place where he or she determines to trust the Lord. Now, this is not to say that

the person will do this perfectly every time, but does he or she ever "mix in" a level of biblical thinking or understanding in this area? Where is the individual's heart in relation to these things? Does he or she talk about or exhibit a desire to trust the Lord when things are not going well? Ask any married couple that you know, and I believe they will agree with the following statement – Your success in marriage is largely going to be based on how well you two handle trails together. Are you both going to go into self-protection mode, which means each one is looking out for THEMSELVES (i.e., a ME-focus), or are both of you or one of you at a time going to remember to encourage one another to trust the Lord TOGETHER (i.e., a WE-focus)? When we do not handle trials well, we typically lash out on the person closest to us, which sadly happens to be our spouse, and this is why this observation is so important.

8. Is the person gracious with others when others mistreat him or her or when others make a mistake? Many people expect or even demand grace when they make mistakes, but it is really ironic that

those same people are often the first people to hammer others when they make mistakes. You, I, and every other person who will ever be married are going to make mistakes - small ones AND big ones. However, consider the following questions. How does the person treat a waiter or waitress if he or she is inattentive to your table when you are out to eat? How does he or she treat "junior" people at the workplace when they make a mistake on an email or proposal? How does the person treat mistakes made by his or her parents or siblings? How does he or she treat his or her friends when the friends make a mistake on scheduling or flat out forget a get-together? As you observe your potential spouse and how he or she treats people who make mistakes, take good notes – this will be the same treatment you will one day receive from him or her.

9. Is the potential spouse in debt? What is his or her money DNA? Just being in debt, per se, does NOT reflect anything positive or negative. However, HOW he or she got into debt may be more telling. If it was through a series of unfortunate events outside of one's control, then this would be a non-issue. Unless the amount

of debt incurred prior to marriage, would impact one's marriage finances. Then it could still be an obstacle. Again, if this is something you are willing to absorb and adjust to, then that is between you, your potential spouse, and the Lord. However, if the debt incurred by your potential spouse is due to a lack of self-control, an immature use of spending to use material things to meet "spiritual needs," an extreme recklessness in risk taking, or just a general lack of responsibility (i.e., he or she did not FEEL like working, so he or she racked up credit card debt while binge-watching Netflix for a year OR something to that effect), then there may be a problem. This could be a serious RED FLAG, especially if the person does NOT recognize that this is a problem and seems content to continue living in this manner. Remember, financial issues are one of the main areas the sin nature will manifest in a marriage. Thus, to see this kind of stark contrast in someone who is a potential spouse should give you great concern about further pursuit of the relationship.

10. Realize that dating and mating are related and not two totally separate things. Single believers should date to find a mate, NOT just date to have fun, to pass time, or to fit in with the rest of the world, secular and Christian! Often, church single groups or college/career age groups resemble the mindset of the "meat market" that happens at many local clubs and bars every weekend. In fact, most dating experiences just help people practice for divorce. Dating basically provides a training academy for doing and learning everything that is opposite of God's original design for marriage. With every partner you date, you are just picking up another three credit hours in your training for future divorce. What do I mean by that? Dating trains you to self-protect and to be completely hidden, disguised, and covered up. Transparency is non-existent because you do not really know the person you are with, so you learn to be very careful with what and how you share. Now, this in and of itself is wise in any relationship in the early stages. The problem is when you stack relationship upon relationship, and you continue in this early-stage mindset in each and every

relationship. It then becomes a hard habit to break in marriage. Dating also trains people how NOT to be dependent upon one another, how NOT to have one-ness, and often tempts people to engage in intimacy even though this is harmful outside of the marriage relationship and apart from God's design.

Ultimately, the summary of the Generic Do's is the following: realize that character is more important than personality and more important than good looks. Some have tended to confuse or equate character and personality, and thus some women think that the ideal husband and spiritual leader is the one with the "salesman-type" personality. They think because he is outgoing, aggressive, and assertive that he is going to be a great husband. Not necessarily! He could be proud, arrogant, and could be selling you on how "spiritual" he is without having one ounce of interest in Jesus Christ. On the flip side, there are some men who are not as outgoing, aggressive, and assertive, which may lead some women to look down upon them as a potential spouse. Additionally, for men, some think that the ideal "submissive" wife is the woman who is shy or passive, but again this in and of itself tells you nothing. In each of these cases, personality has been confused with character. Again, character is what matters – how does your potential spouse respond to the Lord? How does he or she measure up to the ten items previously mentioned?

GENERIC DON'TS IN SPOUSE HUNTING

As with the generic do's list from above, the first and foremost "don't" on this list is don't marry an unbeliever. Do not even consider it! Do not date an unbeliever because, if you are dating, your strategic plan is to find someone that you can marry. It is interesting to consider all the different ways God instructed Israel to be careful about intermarrying with pagan unbelievers. God knew something then that is still true in principle today, and that is there is great influence (for the good or for the bad) involved in a marriage relationship. One of God's greatest communicated concerns about the nation of Israel when they began to settle in the land of Canaan was that the foreign Canaanite people would draw them away from Yahweh. Deuteronomy 7:2-4 says, "And when the LORD your God delivers them over to you, you shall conquer them *and* utterly destroy them. You shall make no covenant with them nor show mercy to them. Nor shall you make marriages with them. You shall not give your daughter to their son, nor take their daughter for your son. For they will turn your sons away from following Me, to serve other gods; so the anger of the LORD will be aroused against you and destroy you suddenly." Assuming that we are on the same page with this common-sense point of not marrying an unbeliever, let's move on to other generic don'ts as you spouse hunt. Again, this is not a comprehensive list, but hopefully it is a helpful list. They are the following.

1. **DO NOT** let the culture squeeze you into its mold regarding relationships, dating, and true love! Romans 12:1-2 says, "I beseech you therefore, brethren, by the mercies of God, that you present your bodies a living sacrifice, holy, acceptable to God, *which is* your reasonable service. And do not be conformed to this world, but be transformed by the renewing of your mind, that you may prove what *is* that good and acceptable and perfect will of God." The word "conformed" means to fashion alike, to conform to the same pattern outwardly.[67] Paul is saying, "Don't be letting the world squeeze you into its mold!" Don't be molded by the mannerisms,

---

[67] Zodhiates, The Complete Word Study New Testament, 4964.

speech, expressions, styles, and habits of this world! Kenneth Wuest has paraphrased the verse as follows: "Stop assuming an outward expression that does not come from within you and is not representative of what you are in your inner being but is patterned after this age; but change your outward expression to one that comes from within and is representative of your inner being, by the renewing of your mind."[68] Additionally, the translation "world" is probably not the best translation here of the word *"aion,"* which means "age, where it refers to an age or time" in contrast to *"kosmos,"* which refers more to people or space.[69] This could be a reference to the sinful world and age we live in, but the application is general enough to apply to the "age" of Christianity that we live in. So, it could be said this way, "Stop being molded by the external and fleeting fashions of this age, whether secular or Christian…" This is an important principle with many applications but

---

[68] George Zeller, "Romans Chapter 12," *Middletown Bible Church*, accessed August 23, 2020, http://www.middletownbiblechurch.org/romans/romans12.htm.
[69] Zodhiates, The Complete Word Study New Testament, 165.

specifically in the area of "spouse hunting." There is often a culture, even within Christendom, of believers trying to speed up the process of dating and mating among young people. Many believers cannot wait to play matchmaker for all the available young and single people in their church. In fact, churches have entire ministries devoted to single young people with a stated, or implied, goal of getting some of these young people into marriage relationships. As a young single person, recognize that many well-intentioned believers will try to "shape you into their mold." Too many believers are influenced by what they see in Hollywood or in Disney or Hallmark movies! Finding a spouse must happen on God's timing and in God's way, and you can trust the Lord for this. You do NOT have to trust a singles group or some worldly, carnal strategy to find a mate. Believers are often molded by the world and begin to think, "If I do not get out there, the Lord cannot bring a person to me. I better join this group, and I better go to this church, and I better join this dating website or app…I better…I better…" Basically, this is just one more area where a single believer who is "spouse hunting" can trust the Lord and stop trusting him or herself!

2. **DO NOT** live together before getting married! Please understand as a young person that this is one of the major ways the age wants to conform and mold you right now. People are functioning according to worldly wisdom, which goes something like this: "We are in love with each other, and we want to get married someday, but we feel like it would be wise and prudent to try it out first, just in case we are seeing it wrong now. Then, if we need to call it off, it will not be a messy divorce." Unfortunately, many people imagine that living together before marriage resembles taking a car for a test drive, but here is the problem with this analogy: The car does not have hurt feelings if the driver dumps it back at the used car lot and decides not to buy it. The analogy works great if you picture yourself as the driver, but it stinks if you picture yourself as the car.[70]

---

[70] Jennifer Roback Morse, "The Problem With Living Together," *Focus on the Family*, last modified January 1, 2001, accessed August 23, 2020, https://www.focusonthefamily.com/marriage/the-problem-with-living-together/.

This is exactly what "cohabitation" does, and it is astonishing to look at some of the more recent statistics on this phenomenon. Today, as many as 70% of first marriages among women aged 18-35 are preceded by cohabitation. They predict that number will reach 80% in the near future.[71] A 2016 Barna study revealed that the majority of Americans (65%) now believe that cohabitation before marriage is a good idea. Especially disturbing in this study is the conclusion that 41% percent of practicing Christians strongly or somewhat strongly agree that cohabitation is a good idea.[72] Even the secular social science data on cohabitation is **very clear**: Cohabitation leads to higher divorce rates after marriage. "People with cohabiting experience who marry have a 50 to 80% higher likelihood of divorcing than married couples who never

---

[71] Scott M. Stanley, "The Risks for Couples Moving In Together," *Psychology Today*, last modified July 10, 2018, accessed August 23, 2020, https://www.psychologytoday.com/us/blog/sliding-vs-deciding/201807/the-risks-couples-moving-in-together.

[72] George Barna, "Majority of Americans Now Believe in Cohabitation," *The Barna Group*, last modified June 24, 2016, accessed August 23, 2020, https://www.barna.com/research/majority-of-americans-now-believe-in-cohabitation/.

cohabited."[73] Ironically, even when cohabitation is agreed upon by both parties, each party tends to view the decision differently. Women tend to view cohabitation as a step **towards** marriage, while men view cohabitation as a compromise to **delay** marriage a little bit more (i.e., it is less of a commitment than marriage). So, the primary argument for cohabitation is completely torn down by empirical data. Cohabitation does not fireproof your marriage, but rather it throws gasoline and a match to it! God's view of marriage is that you get married, and then you become one flesh. Cohabitation does this in reverse – you become one flesh and then **maybe** you'll get married. Hebrews 13:4 says, "Marriage *is* honorable among all, and the bed undefiled; but fornicators and adulterers God will judge." Marriage is honorable "among all" including the Lord, and the "bed undefiled," meaning there is nothing polluted or corrupt with marital intimacy. Sexual intimacy

---

[73] Brett Kunkle and John Stonestreet, A Practical Guide to Culture: Helping the Next Generation Navigate Today's World, (David C. Cook: Colorado Springs, 2017), 173.

is reserved for a marriage relationship, period! Now, there are many who say, "We are just living together, but we are not having any type of sexual intimacy." I just want to say to these people, "Maybe you are living next door to Pollyanna, but I live in the real world, and I know that when you put two people in the same house, who are attracted to one another, the temptation is almost too much to bear." This is an unwise and highly tempting situation that you are putting yourself in should you choose to cohabit. Hebrews 13:4 goes on to say, "But fornicators and adulterers God will judge." So, in contrast to the purity and honorable set-up of marriage and marital intimacy, any sexual intimacy outside of the marriage relationship is defiled, sinful, and will face God's judgment. Now, for the believer in Jesus Christ, the judgment of eternal death (i.e. the lake of fire) is off the table because of the finished work of Christ. However, there are natural consequences, as are described in Galatians 6:7-8. This could include out of wedlock pregnancy, an abusive relationship, and a loss of property/money. There are spiritual consequences, such as loss of fellowship with the Lord, loss of fellowship with other believers, loss of reward, loss of testimony, and potential church discipline (See 1 Corinthians 5). Because ultimately the decision to cohabit for a believer in Jesus Christ is in direct rebellion to and total disregard to God's Word and God's heart on the matter of marriage, the flesh or sin nature becomes the dominating factor in this believer's life. Is it any wonder that researchers at U.C.L.A. found that cohabiters experienced significantly more difficulty in their marriages with adultery, alcohol, drugs and independence than couples who did not cohabit?[74]

3. **DO NOT** cross the steps and stages of physical intimacy too quickly. A snowball once pushed downhill becomes very difficult to stop! Holding hands, embracing, kissing, super-kissing, caressing, super-caressing, more and more, more intense, more and more, and sexual intercourse. A small amount of physical contact always leads to more. Holding hands may be satisfying at first, but soon the

---

[74] Kunkle and Stonestreet, A Practical Guide to Culture, 173.

Spouse Hunting Part 1

novelty and thrill of holding hands will wear off, and there will be a need to go a step further.[75] You may never have desired to go as far as you got, but you got there taking one small step at a time, and you just want to be careful not to cross those steps in the stages of physical intimacy too quickly.

4. **DO NOT** even consider marrying an unbeliever OR a carnal Christian! As mentioned earlier as a "knock-out" factor for marriage, marrying an unbeliever should be completely off the table in your thinking. Again, who in his or her right mind would ever knowingly sign-up for severe pain? Severe heartache? Overwhelming frustration and or hurt? However, if a believer knowingly makes the decision to marry an unbeliever, he or she is signing up for just this type of life! The same is also true of a believer marrying a carnal believer. Although a believer has two *SOURCES* from which they can live life — one *SOURCE* is the sin nature, the

---

[75] George Keller, "Chapter 12: Dating and Waiting," *Middletown Bible Church*, accessed August 23, 2020, http://www.middletownbiblechurch.org/prelatio/pr12.pdf.

flesh, or the indwelling power of sin, and the other *SOURCE* is the Spirit of God – carnal believers are choosing to live life from the *SOURCE* of the flesh. Now, the flesh does NOT improve, even for the believer in Jesus Christ. So, the same list of harmful outcomes from this *SOURCE* of life are still able to manifest themselves in the lives of believers. This means that a believer who is carnal is governed by his or her selfish sin-nature, and that, even in their most pleasant moments, his or her actions, attitudes, and words are all tainted, whether consciously or subconsciously, by impure motives. What believer, who desires God's design and God's best for one's marriage, would sign-up for that? Yet, sadly enough, every believer who chooses to buck the wisdom of the Word of God is signing up for this when he or she chooses to marry a carnal Christian. Again, it may not show up right away, and it may not show up very often, but it is there, always lurking because this is the consistent *SOURCE* from which a carnal believer is living life.

5. **DO NOT** compound mistakes! Believers make mistakes! Even believers whose deepest heart desires are to walk with the Lord and live a life pleasing to Him. Some believers, who have made mistakes, feel like they are now locked into a certain future. If a believer was to lose his or her virginity in a moment of weakness, or even in a moment of bad decision-making, often he or she feels like the ONLY way to make it right is to now marry the person he or she had pre-marital sex with. Moreover, there are often even greater and more lasting consequences than just the guilt of that one act – the young woman in the relationship gets pregnant. In times past, the common wisdom was that if a young man got a young woman pregnant, the honorable thing to do was to get married. Unfortunately, this often compounds the original bad decision. Now, the great thing about the first bad decision is that God takes something that was negative (i.e., pre-marital sex) and turns it into something positive (i.e., the birth of baby). That is a blessing from God, and we can always stand firm that regardless of the decisions that got them to that point, that child is an undisputed

blessing from God! But, you know what that new mother needs more than rushing into a marriage with an unbeliever or a carnal believer? She needs to learn how to walk with the Lord. That child needs a mother who is spiritual and who loves him or her, disciplines him or her, and raises that child with a mindset to fear and trust the Lord. Additionally, that mother needs a man who is pursuing the Lord, who will walk by means of the Spirit in loving her as Christ loved the Church, loving that child and raising that child to love, fear, and trust the Lord. Whether or not it ends up being BOTH or just ONE of the biological parents, this is what the child needs most. The child does not need someone around who is dominated by the sin nature, manifesting the works of the flesh (via verbal, emotional, physical, and maybe even sexual abuse) just because someone feels OBLIGATED to get married to someone who had the ability to get someone pregnant. That is NOT a qualification for a good spouse!

6. **DO NOT** become pressured into doing things that you are uncomfortable doing! In other words, do not violate your own

conscience! If your potential spouse is a person who is constantly pushing you, nagging you, trying to talk you into violating your own conscience, this is a MAJOR red flag! Drop him or her like a rock immediately! This is very serious because if one is doing that, he or she is 100% self-centered and cares little to nothing about your own spiritual health and walk with the Lord. This is NOT the type of person you want to spend the rest of your life with. 1 Timothy 1:18-20 says, "This charge I commit to you, son Timothy, according to the prophecies previously made concerning you, that by them you may wage the good warfare, having faith and a good conscience, which some having rejected, concerning the faith have suffered shipwreck, of whom are Hymenaeus and Alexander, whom I delivered to Satan that they may learn not to blaspheme." When you and I do not "hold on" to a good conscience, we run the risk of shipwrecking our faith. In other words, if you get into the habit of violating your conscience, and a person is encouraging you or even tempting you to do so, you could become stagnant in your relationship to the Lord, and no human relationship is worth that!

7. **DO NOT** have a one-person complex! Even if you like the person a lot, even if you truly believe you love him or her, and you truly believe this person is the one you want to marry, this person should never become the center of your world. That position is ONLY and ALWAYS reserved for Jesus Christ. Unfortunately, a potential spouse can become a huge DISTRACTION from one's spiritual life. Often, in dating relationships, you will see young people interested in spiritual things, and then they find "the one," and they begin to drop out of ministry and drop out of anything that resembles the "one-anothers" of Scripture because they only have eyes and time for their potential spouse. The second that a potential spouse becomes the center of your world, you are setting yourself up for disappointment, frustration, and anxiety, because guess what? That person is **<u>NOT</u>** your Savior, nor can he or she be! The individual is not perfect, and he or she is going to mess up, so if you put him or her on a pedestal, you have taken Jesus Christ off that pedestal. Rest assured, that if you are enamored with one person, you are not thinking biblically. If there is one person to be

enamored with, it is Jesus Christ! He will never disappoint you! He will never let you down! He will always be there for you! It is great that you have potentially found yourself a spouse for life but do yourself and your future spouse a favor – do NOT make them the center of your world. Both you and him or her will benefit most when you are occupied with the Lord Jesus, when He is the center of your focus because then and ONLY then will you be walking by means of the Spirit.

8. **DO NOT** destroy other relationships with your Dad/Mom, family, friends, etc. for a potential spouse! A person who is truly interested in loving you and spending the rest of your life with you will be interested in promoting healthy relationships within your circle of family and friends. If they are NOT…**RUN!** This is a key indicator that he or she is immature, selfish, and dominated by the sin nature. In fact, many abusive-type people want to get you away from your family, so he or she can control you and isolate you. Often it happens without the victim even knowing it until it is too late. The potential spouse can capitalize on everything your family or friends

have done wrong, and he or she can make his or her best effort to set him or herself apart as your one and only Savior, and the ONLY one who truly cares about you and wants your best interests. Anyone who claims to want the best for you will want all your relationships to be healthy and flourishing.

For many Christian young men and young women, they can hardly imagine something worse than being single for their entire lives. This, to them, would be worse than anything they could possibly imagine. However, the truth is the truth — it is better to be single and **ALONE** than to be married to the **WRONG** person. If a Christian young person can trust the Lord Jesus to handle his or her eternal death problem on the cross of Calvary, can the young person also trust Him in providing for a mate or providing for their singleness? Yes, the believer can!

CHAPTER 6
SPOUSE HUNTING PART 2

Behind making the decision to trust in Jesus Christ and His finished work alone for your salvation, who you decide to marry will be the most important decision you make in your life on this earth. In the last chapter, we considered some generic dos and don'ts for spouse hunting. In this chapter, much like a funnel, which is wide at the top and narrow at the bottom, we want to continue giving guidelines for funneling your options down farther. Spouse hunting starts with the entire human race and slowly funnels itself down to a small handful of people. Is he or she a believer? Is he or she desiring to walk with the Lord? What is his or her personality like? Are you attracted to him or her? Do you share common interests? How does he or she handle trials? These are all funneling observations at some level, and each stage and level help to narrow one's options. Now, is there a "one" for each individual believer? We should save that debate for another time, so for now, let's consider some more specific ways to funnel down the options for a spiritually minded believer to marry. It should be mentioned that in spouse hunting, you are **NOT** looking for perfection! Perfection does **NOT** exist! What you are looking for is consistency or growth in character, a direction of heart, and self-awareness and personal responsibility when one's response is sinful, carnal, and immature.

Let's be honest, nobody comes right out and says during the dating process, "Before you get serious about me, I just want you to know that I am going to be a terrible spouse. I am completely selfish. I do not want to grow spiritually. My view of marriage is through the lens of me being the center every time. I will not love you well, and I will probably criticize you in public every chance I get. When you upset me, I am going to scream at you and belittle you. I am going to manipulate you to get my way, and then I will expect you to sleep next to me at night and provide intimacy for me when I desire it. Are you O.K. with that?" Nobody says that, right! Everyone tries to put his or her best foot forward, and I think everyone wants to be something more than he or she is presently. However, when you are choosing a spouse, you must be observant. You must be willing to walk away when you see certain "knock-out" factors. You must be willing to put on your detective hat and attempt to sniff out things that are not readily apparent on the surface. You may not be able to know everything about a potential spouse, but you can observe things that give you an indication of what **SOURCE** he or she is living his or her life from. In this chapter, we want to consider some specific "no no's" for Christian men and Christian women as they filter through the spousal options available. These "no no's" are indicators that the potential mate is living from the **SOURCE** of the sin nature.

FOR MEN (SOME NO NO'S ABOUT WOMEN)

1. **Beware of a contentious woman** – Let's consider the following three verses. Proverbs 21:9 says, "Better to dwell in a corner of a housetop, than in a house shared with a contentious woman." Proverbs 21:19 says, "Better to dwell in the wilderness, than with a contentious and angry woman. Proverbs 25:24 says, "*It is* better to dwell in a corner of a housetop, than in a house shared with a contentious woman. The word translated "contentious" means

strife, dissension, or a verbal quarrel.[76] It describes a woman who is a source or object of contention as an established character quality. Notice the progression here as well as the face that Solomon tells his son that it is better to live three other places than with a quarreling wife. These places are: (1) A corner of your house – This is exactly what many married men do. They find something to do in the garage or the shed, and they do it either intentionally or unintentionally to get away from their contentious wife, (2) On the corner of your roof – This movement represents being either farther away from one's wife than the garage or shed mentioned earlier, and (3) Out in the desert – Again, this represents a progression of being even farther away from her. This progression communicates something a man must realize – living with a contentious woman is unbearable torture! This is actually how Solomon describes it as the following in Proverbs 19:13, "A foolish

---

[76] James A. Swanson, Dictionary of Biblical Languages with Semantic Domains : Hebrew (Old Testament), (Oak Harbor: Logos Research Systems, Inc., 1997), Electronic ed., 4506.

son *is* the ruin of his father, and the contentions of a wife *are* a continual dripping." Solomon goes on to say in Proverbs 27:15-16 that you cannot stop it. He states, "A continual dripping on a very rainy day and a contentious woman are alike; whoever restrains her restrains the wind, and grasps oil with his right hand." So, what does this look like practically? Maybe you go to a restaurant with her, and all she does is complain about the waitress and complain about the food. In a hostile way, she sends the food back. Now, I am not saying she can never complain or be disappointed with the service in a restaurant, but I am saying that if this is ALL she does everywhere you go, then this could be an indicator and this is just the beginning. She is contentious at the dry cleaner, at the grocery store, with her parents, with her siblings, with her employees, with her friends, with her boss, and with everyone else BUT YOU currently! If she is quarreling in almost every sphere of her life, and she seems to always be looking for a fight, then guess what? That will translate to you one day, and you will fight the natural urge in your marriage to distance yourself from this toxic woman. As in any other area of carnality, by continuing to pursue a contentious woman, you are knowingly signing up for a lifetime of potential misery. It is better to recognize it now, before you are married, and move on.

2. **Beware of JUST a beautiful or charming woman** – What we learn from life, and what we learn from the Scriptures is that beautiful women are a dime a dozen! There are many beautiful women in this world. Now, this is NOT to say that you need to marry someone to whom you are not attracted. As a young Christian, when I started getting serious about walking with the Lord, I had a misconception in this area. I thought, "Well, if I am going to marry a Christian girl, I am just going to have to marry this nerd, who is reading her Bible all the time, who has warts and moles all over her face, and who is going to be 800 pounds overweight." I guess I thought that would be really spiritual of me! I believe God wants us to have the entire package — a woman who we are attracted to AND a woman who is pursuing deeper fellowship with Jesus Christ. Many guys get distracted by beauty, which is what we

want to guard against. Do not just go for a girl if she has one of the two things you are looking for – find the whole package! By the way, as a side note for the ladies, everything being said here is just the opposite for you. What I mean by that is do not just be the girl that focuses on her looks! That is what the world does. That is worldly and carnal thinking. Be the type of woman that is the whole package for a man. Start today pursuing deeper fellowship with the Lord and be aware that out of the two things mentioned as a whole package, this is the much more valuable one to a man who is also pursuing deeper fellowship with the Lord. Proverbs 31:30 says, "Charm *is* deceitful and beauty *is* passing, but a woman *who* fears the LORD, she shall be praised." To say that "charm is deceitful," Solomon is saying that certain women can put on the charm thicker than syrup. The charm can come in such a way that you cannot even see it. Some women know what to say, how to say it, how to smile when they say it, how to wink or bat their eyes when they say it, and how to manipulate and get their way. Many women, even carnal believers who are women, have perfected this mode of manipulation. This, again, is another reason why you should listen to your friends and family when they verbalize concerns regarding your potential spouse, whether she is your girlfriend or your fiancé already. This, too, is why it is **NOT** wise to get engaged and then introduce your fiancé to Mom and Dad, your other friends, and your other family members. You really put them in an awkward situation if you are that far along in the relationship before they have had a chance to provide you with loving input. Young men, please be aware of a simple fact – you may not be seeing the "real" her, and you NEED to see the "real" her before you say I do. Sometimes your family and friends can see things you will not because they are not going to be distracted by her eyes, her smile, her makeup, or how cute she looks in a pair of jeans! You have the ability to be distracted, and your family and friends will be less distracted than you. The second thing that Solomon says in Proverbs 31:30 is that "beauty is passing." The word translated "passing" comes from the word meaning idol or a fashioned object with a focus on its lack of value, meaningless, emptiness, futility, uselessness.[77] The fact is that beauty gets you absolutely nowhere in the day-to-day trenches of doing life. When your car breaks down, you cannot just send your wife out there in her white dress and have the car fix itself. Beauty does not help with trials, difficult circumstances, or one's relationship with the Lord. You need a woman that is going to trust the Lord and encourage you to trust the Lord. When you are naturally bent to start relying upon your own ingenuity and all your self-reliant strategies for living life, you need a woman who is going to boldly say to you, "Honey, we need to trust the Lord in this! We need to wait on the Lord! Let's pray about this! Let's encourage each other in the Lord!" This is the kind of woman you want, and this is the kind of woman you need – not someone who just looks good in makeup or has a pretty smile – someone who has depth to her and someone who is consistently pursuing the Lord. In fact, for some women, beauty often causes them to become more self-focused, and it can actually be a

---

[77] Swanson, DBL Hebrew, 2039.

hindrance in their relationship with the Lord and others. For some women, physical beauty is an obstacle to be overcome in their spiritual lives, and many are never able to do it. Young men need to be extremely observant here – what is this woman's energy and pursuit spent on? Pursuing the Lord or pursuing or pampering her physical beauty?

3. **Beware of a disrespectful woman** – Solomon does not hold back in his description of this type of woman in Proverbs 12:4 when he says, "An excellent wife *is* the crown of her husband, but she who causes shame *is* like rottenness in his bones." In the phrase "She who causes shame is like rottenness in his bones," the word translated "causes shame" means to humiliate, to bring shame, or cause disgrace.[78] Notice closely where this shame destroys a man – it is like "rottenness in his bones." That means that this type of treatment from a potential spouse destroys him from within. It damages him internally, crushes his spirit, and tears him down. As

---

[78] Swanson, DBL Hebrew, 1017.

a result, he becomes a shell of the man he could have become. Whether you realize it or not, young man, you will NEED respect and honor from your wife in marriage. There will be times in your life that the most valuable thing you need is NOT a raise or promotion at work, recognition and approval from your colleagues, and popularity amongst your friends. NO, the most important thing, the most valuable thing you will need is the support, respect, and honor from your wife. With this you can bust through brick walls! Without it, your bones will crumble and rot away inside of you. So, how does this work out practically, and how can you notice this before you say I do? Pay close attention to how she treats her father, her grandfather, or her brothers. Does she roll her eyes when they speak? Does she cut them off or discount everything they say? Does she give eye contact to them when they are speaking to her, or does she rudely do other things? Rest assured, you will most likely get the same treatment at some point. Additionally, watch closely how her mother treats her father. Although many girls can grow spiritually and should not be held accountable for their mothers' sins, many girls simply repeat what they have seen. Unless they are aware that this is a potential blind spot for them, they could naturally pick up the sinful tendencies of their mothers. This again has the potential to be an obstacle to you growing and becoming the man that God has called you to be.

4. **Beware of an undiscerning woman** – Proverbs 11:22 says, "*As a ring of gold in a swine's snout, so is a lovely woman who lacks discretion.*" The word translated "discretion" here means discernment or good judgment as a facet of wisdom and capacity for understanding.[79] So, what you are looking for guys is a woman who learns from her mistakes. She does not just "plow ahead," doing the same wrong, carnal things and then expect different results. That is **NOT** wisdom! You can see this in someone with whom you are attending Bible study or with someone who studies the Bible and learns all of this biblical truth but just has zero ability to apply the truth she has learned. Then, when confronted with the

---

[79] Swanson, DBL Hebrew, 3248.

connection, she justifies her actions and attitudes because that is just how she feels. She consistently rejects the concept of the Bible instructing and/or correcting her. Interestingly enough, the word translated "discretion" is also used of taste buds in order to describe the ability to distinguish and enjoy flavor in foods or drinks. Imagine going through life eating food and having no ability to distinguish and enjoy flavor – that would be torture! Yet, this is the word used to describe this type of woman. She has no ability to distinguish spiritual from carnal, right from wrong, and she will handle conflict immaturely and justify her attitudes and actions. She is unable to recognize or even realize that she has blind spots. This type of woman has absolutely zero discernment. Solomon clearly does not mince words with this! According to Solomon, this type of woman is just like putting a ring of gold in a pig's nose. We might say it is like putting lipstick on a pig – it takes the loveliness away from her.

FOR WOMEN (SOME <u>NO NO'S</u> ABOUT GUYS)

1. **Beware of a lazy or unfaithful man who is unwilling to sacrifice**

    a. *Lazy* — Unfortunately, for women, there are many lazy men in existence today. What makes many of them so dangerous is that they are really good at convincing a woman that they are **NOT** lazy! Proverbs 12:11 addresses this type of man when it says, "He who tills his land will be satisfied with bread, but he who follows frivolity *is* devoid of understanding." Solomon provides us with two contrasts here: **First**, the one who "tills his land will be satisfied with bread." The word translated "tills" means to expend considerable energy and intensity in a task or function.[80] Remember, in Solomon's time, working was largely described in agricultural terms, as it takes discipline and a lot of hard work to be a successful farmer. Farmers, even in our day, do not just show up to a field, throw a couple of seeds in the ground, show up once a week to water it, and then show up again three

---

[80] Swanson, DBL Hebrew, 6268.

months later to pick it out of the ground. It takes much more work than that. In fact, it is back-breaking, moment-by-moment work to care for crops and seeing them to harvest. So, this passage is describing a hard-working man who receives the benefit from his hard work. The next phrase says that he is "satisfied with bread," which describes a state of physical contentment.[81] So, this man, via his hard work, provides for all of his own needs. Thus, the implication is that this type of man will take care of his responsibilities. He is NOT going to be a young guy mooching off his mom and dad. He is taking initiative and is not expecting mom or dad to bail him out of his bad decisions. He is not looking to the government through its entitlement programs. He is not milking some system, figuring out how long he can collect unemployment before he has to go back to work again, rather he is proactively working to provide for himself. Now, the **second** description we have

---

[81] Swanson, DBL Hebrew, 8425.

in this verse represents the flip side of this equation. The passages says the one "who follows frivolity, is devoid of understanding." The word translated "frivolity" means vain things, empty things, worthless things.[82] Additionally, the word "follows" means to pursue or to chase hard after.[83] So, this is not just someone who likes to have fun and goof off once in a while, but rather someone who pursues this as the course of his life. Now, I want to be careful not to go too far in our applications here, but let me put it this way – if a grown man only wants to do fun things with his free time all the time, that may describe this man. If he is a grown man and still playing ten hours a day of video games, if he is in his forties and still pursuing a music career with his band, if he is hunting ten to fifteen weekends a year, if he spends hours upon hours brewing his own hand-crafted beer, then he may be this man. Again, it

---

[82] Swanson, DBL Hebrew, 8199.
[83] Swanson, DBL Hebrew, 8103.

is not that hobbies are BAD. That is **NOT** what this verse is saying at all. It is saying that this type of man "chases hard" after these things, meaning they are a major focus for him and a major description of what makes him, him. His mindset is "fun-fun-fun" – Six Flags every day and pizza every night! The problem with this mindset is that when the Spirit of God wants to direct his focus, it will be focused on the Lord Jesus AND on other people. The Spirit of God will want to direct that man's thinking towards fulfilling the "one anothers" of Scripture. The Spirit of God will want to direct his thinking to his wife, his kids, his neighbors, and his church body. If this man is devoting all of his energy to his own "fun" as a way of life, it is an indication that he is not spiritually minded. Solomon goes on to say that this man is "devoid of understanding," meaning he lacks a true compass. Literally, the phrase could read, "he lacks or is without heart." The things he gets excited about will end up harming him and everyone around him.

Proverbs 21:25 says, "The desire of the lazy *man* kills him, for his hands refuse to labor."

b. *Faithfulness* – It is ironic that this is the one character quality emphasized more than any other when it comes to being a disciple of Jesus Christ. 1 Corinthians 4:1-2 says, "Let a man so consider us, as servants of Christ and stewards of the mysteries of God. Moreover it is required in stewards that one be found **faithful**." Additionally, when Paul instructs Timothy in 2 Timothy 2:2 on the type of man he should invest his time in, he states, "And the things that you have heard from me among many witnesses, commit these to **faithful** men who will be able to teach others also." Fortunately, for women who are spouse-hunting, observing faithfulness is fairly simple: Does he do what he says he is going to do? Does he show up when he says he is going to show up? Does he listen and stay engaged with you? Does he ask and stay abreast of your likes, dislikes, and fears or concerns? Does he keep his commitments to others? Some men are good at keeping their commitments to YOU during the courtship phase, but it is telling if they do not keep their commitment to others. This will be YOU one day, and you will most likely receive this type of treatment if and when he decides he no longer needs to impress you. Can you trust him with sensitive information? These are all very practical questions, which provide potential areas to observe in a prospective spouse. Proverbs 25:19 says, "Confidence in an unfaithful *man* in time of trouble i*s like* a bad tooth and a foot out of joint." The word "confidence" here means security, safety, free from danger, and it implies reliance upon someone or something.[84] Unfaithful men cannot be relied upon when you need them the most. This is what makes an unfaithful man an unattractive life partner – life is full of trials, and you need to rely upon someone from time to time. If he is unreliable, it will only add to your level of frustration. Solomon goes on to describe what relying upon an unfaithful man is like with two practical illustrations.

---

[84] Swanson, DBL Hebrew, 4440.

First, he likens it to "a bad tooth," which cannot bite down on food like it normally can and, thus, is unreliable. Anyone who has had a loose tooth or any kind of dental pain can relate to this comment. Imagine biting into an apple with a loose or sore tooth! Basically, when a tooth is like this, you cannot use it. Secondly, he likens depending upon an unfaithful man to a "foot out of joint." What happens when a person is running or walking, and he or she puts his or her entire body weight on a bum foot? He or she falls to the ground. Even though the foot is still on the body, it is practically unusable. So, how much faithfulness are you looking for? Over 50%? Over 75%? Well, take the two daily examples that Solomon gives and ask yourself the following questions: (1) If my tooth only hurt 25% of the time, but the other 75% of the time I could count on it, would I still avoid that side of my mouth when I am chewing? (2) If my foot only gave out on me 25% of the time, but the other 75% of the time it could hold my weight, how often would I still avoid putting all my weight on that foot? You see, faithfulness does NOT get better in degrees, but it must be a stable, valued character trait of a man who is controlled by the Spirit of God. He may have lapses from time to time, but, for the most part, he is dependable because he values and sees value in being faithful in his life. The problem for most people, men included, is if they are consistently unfaithful in certain areas of life, they will most likely be unfaithful in other areas. In other words, unfaithfulness does NOT just limit itself to forgetting to take out the garbage or being late for dinner appointments – it can translate in a lot more damaging areas (i.e., sexual infidelity, financial infidelity, deceitful cover-ups, etc.).

c. *Unwilling to Sacrifice* – If a potential husband is unwilling to sacrifice in the dating relationship, that is potentially a big RED flag because of what Ephesians 5:25 teaches. It states, "Husbands, love your wives, just as Christ also loved the Church and gave Himself for her." Now, we will go into much more detail on this passage (Ephesians 5:25-33) in a later chapter, but for now consider how Jesus Christ "loved" the

Church – He did so by sacrificing His very life for her. We also learn from this passage farther down in verse 28 that husbands ought to love their own wives as their own bodies because they are ONE FLESH. So, how does this show up in a potential spouse? Here are a couple of practical questions: (1) Do you always have to do things that he wants to do in the way that he wants to do it? Are you always going out to eat where he wants to go? Are you always doing the activities he wants to do? Does he show any interest in your interests or are you the one always taking up his hobbies and interests to spend more time with him. Trust me, he can survive a few hours in Jo-Ann Fabrics, Hobby Lobby, Wal-Mart, or wherever else you might like to go. (2) If something is important to you, does he make every effort to accommodate your desire? Why wouldn't he accommodate the things that are important to you if they are within his power to do so? If he is a spiritually minded man, even if what is important to you does not make sense to him, he will make an effort to accomplish your desire. In fact, if he is a spiritually minded man, this should be the way he responds to his parents, his siblings, his friends, his co-workers, etc. His mindset is that he can be put out for somebody else, and he is okay with that if it is of benefit to others. (3) Is he willing to sacrifice his "free" time to help you with something, or is his free time sacred? If you attempt to interject yourself into his free time or try to utilize some of it, does it result in World War III? Ladies, trust me, the Bible says you are worth sacrificing for and every one of your human fathers would say, "Amen!" to that. Now, at the same time, you do not want to dominate every second of his free time or expect that you now OWN every second of his free time, but a sacrificial man, empowered by the Spirit of God, is willing to give of his free time when it is important. (4) Does he prioritize your schedule when he is making his own? Does he take into consideration your schedule? This is a major area of conflict in marriage, especially if you are both lone rangers, doing your own thing, whenever you want to do it. If he expects you to change and alter your schedule to fit his, this is a good indicator that he is unwilling to sacrifice for you, and that is a potential RED flag.

2. **Beware of a Harsh-Tongued Man**

    a. *He Uses Destructive Words* – Proverbs 15:4 says, "A wholesome tongue is a tree of life, but perverseness in it breaks the spirit." The word "perverseness" means falsehood or deceit.[85] These are spoken words that are crooked and perverted from the truth and so are false. The way this works out in day-to-day life, especially as it relates to looking for a husband, is to recognize that there are some men who can take any situation in life and spin it in such a way that makes them look good and makes you look bad. They can flip the facts in a case and make you feel like trash and make them look like God's gift to planet earth. The tragedy of this is that this type of communication does NOT happen in a vacuum and does NOT happen without any harsh consequences. There is a way with crooked, perverse words that

---

[85] Swanson, DBL Hebrew, 6157.

cause a person to want to give up and quit. These words can actually "break" someone's spirit. The word translated "breaks" in this verse means to cripple or to cause an ongoing injury that simply fractures you.[86] The old saying, "Sticks and stones may break my bones, but words will never hurt me," is one of the most untrue statements ever uttered and repeated. Words do hurt, crush, destroy, and, according to this verse, cause ongoing fractures. Unfortunately, this happens often in marriages – no physical abuse occurs, but a lot of verbal, emotional "perverseness" does occur. How can you keep an eye out for this? Pay attention to how he treats the women in his life. Look at his grandma, his mom, his sisters, his aunts – whoever is in his life. Notice how they interact with him. Has he broken their spirits? How do they interact with him? Do they try to avoid as much contact with him as possible? Do they seem quieter, subdued, or withdrawn around him? If you see this in a

---

[86] Swanson, DBL Hebrew, 8691.

prospective spouse, address it with him and recognize this as a potential RED flag.

b. *He Does Not Use Wholesome Words* – We skipped over the first part of Proverbs 15:4, which describes a contrast to the perverse tongue, by describing a "wholesome tongue." The word "wholesome" means calmness, composure, or an attitude and/or behavior, which is not harsh in word or deed.[87] In other words, there is a loving and gentle way to communicate with someone that builds him or her up even when having to challenge or confront him or her about something. Even when someone disagrees with you, he or she is still loving, gentle, and calm in his or her communication with you. This is healthy communication and reflects a man who is walking by means of the Spirit. This is communication that desires your best and your growth – **NOT** winning an argument against you or putting you in your place!

---

[87] Swanson, DBL Hebrew, 5341.

3. **Beware of a Deceitful Man**

   a. *Look for a man who tells the truth* – Proverbs 19:1 says, "Better *is* the poor who walks in his integrity than *one who is* perverse in his lips and is a fool." The phrase, "One who is perverse in his lips," literally means someone who is morally crooked or warped through distortion of facts. This type of person is described as a fool. Do you know that some guys actually take pride in this "skill" and how much they can get away with? They have a way of spinning facts to benefit themselves instead of just giving the whole truth. They warp their words to skew situations every chance they get in order to score some points or get some thrill with what they can achieve through deception. They view it as a great accomplishment in using deceit to talk down their bill, get out of a jam, get an item for free through deception (like dessert at Chili's when its NOT his birthday), get an extension on an assignment, and get an excused absence from work when they should not have. It could be small, insignificant things, but, if he is okay with that type of deceit, and, if there is a consistency to his behavior, this could be a red flag for you. Remember, if he does it to others NOW, he will most likely transfer his behavior to you because this is exposing a manifestation of his flesh. Thus, in the future, if your prospective spouse walks according to the flesh, it would logically follow that one way his flesh will go on manifesting itself is through deceitfulness. In the phrase that we skipped over in Proverbs 19:1, we read "Better is the poor who walks in his integrity," meaning life is much simpler when you tell the truth. If a man simply does what he says he is going to do, accepts the consequences for any mistake, and owns up to any potential consequences, life will just be easier for him.

b. *Look for a man that can admit when he is wrong* – Proverbs 28:13 says, "He who covers his sins will not prosper, but whoever confesses and forsakes *them* will have mercy." The word translated "covers" means to intentionally hide from or conceal from others,[88] and the one who does this will not succeed or accomplish anything. This is talking about accountability. Again, you will never find a perfect or fully spiritually mature young person. However, you are looking for someone who recognizes the value of accountability for his actions and comes clean when he does realize he has done something wrong. In essence, you are looking for a man who is looking to actually BE spiritual, NOT just LOOK spiritual! There is a difference! You do not want to be tied up with someone who is a professional cover up artist because ultimately he or she is only deceiving himself. A person who covers up his sins is typically someone who is trying to appear to be something he is not – a true phony, imposter, and hypocrite. This should frighten you because you can never really know if you "really" know this person. This covering up of his sins is intentional, and thus the cover up is actually worse than the initial sin. The initial sin

---

[88] Swanson, DBL Hebrew, 4059.

could have been an accidental sin, or a sin engaged in during a moment of weakness, but cover up takes thought, intentionality, and purposeful deceit. This is why a person like this cannot succeed, and, if you are married to someone like this, he will take you down like an anchor on a boat. If you are married to someone like this, you will be drawn into his web of deceit and phoniness because his only goal in life is to "look good" to others even if internally he is a wreck. If you see this consistently in a potential spouse, you need to move on. You do not need to babysit or cover for a phony, you do not need to babysit or cover for a hypocrite, and you do not need to babysit or cover for an imposter. This type of man will be more concerned about "looking" like a good husband to others than actually "being" a good husband to you.

4. **Beware of a Proud Man**

    a. *Look for a man who values and is willing to listen to counsel* – Proverbs 12:15 says, "The way of a fool *is* right in his own eyes, but he who heeds counsel *is* wise." What is so fascinating about this verse is that it teaches that every decision a fool makes is with the belief that his way is the "right" way every time! He actually has that level of overconfidence and arrogance to think that he makes the right decision every time. Wow, to believe that one is right every time is the epitome of foolishness, and yet many men are this way. Although they would never admit it, and many would verbally admit that they are NOT right all the time, they live out their lives as if they were. As mentioned earlier, many people confuse personality with character, and they mistake perceived "strength" and "confidence" for absolute foolishness. Some of the most confident people in life are some of the biggest fools because they do not know that they do not know! This type of attitude is easily observable in a potential spouse, and definitely something you should keep an eye out for. Also, in line with this is the second phrase in this verse in contrast to the "know it all" fool, which says "but he who heeds counsel is wise." The word translated "heeds" means to hear with the desire to process the information,[89] and why is that such a good thing? This type of response shows that this person does not believe that he knows everything, and he takes a position of a humble learner, someone who desires to learn from O.P.E. (or other people's experience). Some very practical things that you can observe: (1) Does this guy have older, more mature men in his life that he listens to and checks in with? (2) Is he willing to be humble and recognize that he might not be seeing everything correctly? (3) When he is making difficult decisions, does he check with a mentor or someone he views as wise, or does he just blow out of the gate making decisions, never checking with any of his authority structures? This does NOT mean that he has to do everything his mentors or authority structures tell him to do, but the question is – does he even value their opinion, and is it a PART of his decision-making processes? This is important because there is nothing

---

[89] Swanson, DBL Hebrew, 9048.

weak with getting counsel on life decisions! (See 2 Chronicles 20:1-12).

b. *Proud men are resisted by God* – In the Book of Proverbs, there is a direct connection between the pride of a man and his true success in life (See Proverbs 15:25, 33; 16:18-19; 18:12; 29:23). Because we know from Hebrews 11:6 that "without faith it is impossible to please God," we understand that a proud man is NOT a man who walks by faith. However, that is NOT true! The proud man walks by faith – faith in himself! He has faith in his abilities, faith in his ingenuity, faith in his creativity to solve problems, faith in his goodness, faith in his stability, and faith in his character. The proud man's problem is that his faith is in the wrong OBJECT. He places too much confidence in the wrong OBJECT (himself) and does NOT place any faith in the right OBJECT (the Lord Jesus Christ). Being proud is NOT honoring to the Lord, and it reveals that a Christian man is out of fellowship with the Lord. Again, consistently carnal men do

NOT make good prospective spouses, and they make even worse husbands.

c. *Proud men are NOT willing to take and receive correction* – This was spoken of at length in chapter 5, but, as a reminder, this speaks to a man's humility (i.e., recognizing he could be wrong). If he realizes that he could be wrong, he is generally more open to correction, which proves he is NOT stupid (Proverbs 12:1)

CHAPTER 7
HOW TO BE A BIBLICAL HUSBAND PART 1

Every successful team in the history of the world is comprised of individual people, performing their individual roles, and this ensures the great achievement. Each individual functions in different roles, doing his or her part, for the success of the team. Marriage is NO different! On this team, the husband has a role, and the wife has a role. Each of these roles, and their fulfillment, are ultimately done without dependence upon the other person to do his or her role. As with any team, the minute a person stops doing his or her role and begins to focus on another person's role, the team falls into disarray. Although the roles in a marriage are different, the intrinsic value and worth of each person are completely the same before the Lord. Obviously, this is different in the sports world, as quarterbacks are paid more than offensive linemen. However, in marriage, both spouses are loved, valued, and accepted just the way they are IN Christ. Both spouses have had their sins paid for by and through the finished work of Jesus Christ, both spouses have been given every spiritual blessing in heavenly places IN Christ, and both spouses have the indwelling Holy Spirit as a part of those blessings. They have a lot in common!

Even science data tells us that spouses are basically the same. More than 99% of male and female genetic coding is exactly the same. Out of the 30,000 genes in the human genome, the less than 1% variation between the sexes is small. But that percentage difference influences **every single cell in our bodies** – from the nerves that register pleasure and pain to the neurons that transmit perception, thoughts, feelings, and emotions.[90] So, husbands and wives are basically the same – yet also entirely different! Tell me something I do not know, right?

However, when we get to the marriage relationship, the roles must be performed in a certain way from a certain life SOURCE in order for things to function biblically. J. Hampton Keathley IV, a writer and website designer for Bible.org, says, "Both husband and wife must put themselves in a vulnerable position, out of love and trust in God's Word, in order to

---

[90] Curt Hamner et al., Marriage: Its Foundation, Theology, and Mission in a Changing World, (Chicago: Moody Publishers, 2018), 143.

make marriage successful. It involves giving up your patterns of self-protection!"[91] Unfortunately, many people train their whole lives learning how to protect themselves. Many will not put themselves "out there" too much in case their head gets chopped off – "I am not going to apologize to them, because if I do, they will take advantage of me going forward," – "I am not going to tell them I love them first, because I do not want to be embarrassed if they do not reciprocate," – "I am not going to say I want to spend more time with them because what if they do not want to spend more time with me?" Thus, we learn to self-protect, and we take this attitude into our marriage relationships. We look out for number one, and we attempt to protect our emotions and feelings, and we try to prevent ourselves from getting hurt. As a result, we push our spouse away, and often they begin to see us go into "self-protect" mode, and they feed off that and go into the same mode. This is an attitude and mindset that individuals must give up and reject if they desire to fulfill their biblical roles as outlined

---

[91] Hampton Keathley IV, "Love Your Wife Sacrificially (Ephesians 5:25-27)," Bible.org, last modified May 21, 2004, accessed November 17, 2020, https://bible.org/article/love-your-wife-sacrificially-ephesians-525-27.

in Scripture. Instead of trusting in one's own ability to self-protect, the Bible encourages that person to trust in the living God and His methods for a successful marriage.

One of those methods or areas of focus is on one's own role within a marriage relationship. Nowhere in Scripture do the biblical authors emphasize the "rights" of husbands and wives, BUT rather they do note the "roles" or "duties" of husbands and wives. Most marriages with issues find either both or one of the spouses more concerned about their rights than their duties! For instance, many men know Ephesians 5:22 better than they know Ephesians 5:25, and many women know Ephesians 5:25 better than they know Ephesians 5:22. In other words, each spouse spends more time and energy focused on how the other person is NOT fulfilling his or her role or duty. The spouse tends to focus on his or her own "rights" and how they are not being extended to him or her. He or she is more focused on what he or she is entitled to rather than being occupied with his or her God-given role in the marriage. Before the Lord, both husbands and wives are to live and function according to their God-given roles, but only by means of the Spirit.

How to be a Biblical Husband Part 1

So, having introduced the topic of roles and duties within a marriage, we start with the HUSBAND because he is the head of the home. He is designed to be the leader, the proactive initiator, and ultimately the buck stops with him. This may be why there are 9 verses for him in Ephesians 5 and only 3 for his wife! Many marriages fail because the husband does NOT know HOW to lead biblically, or he refuses to be a biblical leader. One respected Bible teacher, commentator, and former pastor was known to say, "85% of the problems in marriage can be traced to the husband's fault."[92] Whether or not that percentage is technically accurate, the point is well taken. Problems with teams generally reflect problems in leadership. Now, wives have their own responsibility, which we will address when we get to their section, BUT many wives have nothing to respond to because their husbands do not lead biblically.

Because of this, it is really tempting to jump right into Ephesians 5:25 because it is a command to husbands to love their wives. We could rush in and tell husbands how bad they are doing at this and how they need to start

---

[92] Keathley, "Love Your Wife."

buying their wives flowers and massage their feet. We can tell them they need to do a better job completing their wives' "to-do lists," how they need to kiss their wives every day, and how they need to tell her they love her every day. However, before we get to the instruction for HUSBANDS in verse 25, we must first understand the assumed resources for HUSBANDS described in verse 18. We must first understand the "toolshed" full of tools available for the HUSBANDS' use in executing their role efficiently.

Imagine for a moment that you, as a good neighbor, volunteered to cut my lawn for me while I was out of town. Let's say I own a couple of acres, but I assure you that the tools you need are in my backyard shed. When you open my backyard shed, you see a shed full of tools, and the first sharp thing you come across is a scalpel. Well, a scalpel could cut some grass, but it may take you days or weeks to cut the grass with a scalpel. It would NOT be very effective or efficient, and, quite frankly, by the time you finished, you would need to start over again because the grass would have grown back a little. The same would be true for the hunting knife you see in there, and the pair of scissors you see, so you keep looking. Finally, you see a push mower, and, although not ideal, this is definitely the best tool you have seen so far. As you begin to consider grabbing it and pulling it out to get started, you look further back in the toolshed, and you see a tarp covering something. You figure since you are in the shed, you might as well look at what is under the tarp. Low and behold, it is a brand-new riding lawn mower! So, you clear space and drive it straight out of the shed and finish mowing your neighbor's lawn within a couple of hours. It's a piece of cake with the right resource! Likewise, husbands must understand the "tools" they possess, which are based upon their position in Jesus Christ, and we find their version of the "riding mower" in verse 18, which is SO KEY to our context when we get to verse 25 and following. Men have divine resources at their disposal, and this is why God can give husbands an impossible command to obey in Ephesians 5:25.

Ephesians 5:18 reads, "And do not be drunk with wine, in which is dissipation; but be filled with the Spirit." There are 3 commands that govern this entire section from verses 18-33: (1) Be **FILLED** with the Spirit, (2) Wives, **SUBMIT** to your own husbands, and (3) Husbands, **LOVE** your wives. In fact, the first command "Be **FILLED** with the Spirit" sets the stage for everything that follows describing inter-personal relationships all the way down to 6:9. Paul sets up this command to be filled with the Spirit by giving a negative command, using a very common and practical example to describe what he means. Ironically, the example he uses is a very licentious example that most people in most time periods can understand. Paul tells them, "Do not be drunk with wine," which is a negated present tense command. In other words, this has some intensity to it! It could mean "Stop an action already in progress," OR "Do not even begin this action." Also, because the command is in the **passive voice**, it indicates that Paul's readers were not to allow wine to act upon them. In other words, do not let wine (and the intake of it) influence you! One thing is certain about wine or any other alcoholic beverage — certain levels of them will ACT on you, guaranteed! This is not something that can be stopped once taken in! Thus, the illustration is clear, and so is the outcome of being drunk with wine. Paul calls it "dissipation," which is a compound word (**a** – negation, and **sozo** – to save or deliver) meaning having no hope of safety.[93] The word "dissipation" came to mean a prodigal, one who spends too much or slides

---

[93] Zodhiates, The Complete Word Study Dictionary, 810.

easily under the fatal influence of others, temptations, and in this case, alcohol. Most people have seen others under the influence of alcohol. There is a certain sense that they are being controlled or influenced by the alcoholic beverage. Alcohol impacts their speech, their physical movements, their choice of activities, their thinking, their restraint through relaxed inhibitions, and their practical wisdom. As a result, they typically engage in risky and or dangerous behavior, and thus, if left to themselves, they could not "save themselves" from the consequences of their reckless behavior.

In stark contrast, but yet still similar, Paul commands believers to "be filled with the Spirit." In other words, don't do this (get drunk with wine), but definitely do this (be filled with the Spirit)! In the same way that a drunk person is impacted and influence by alcohol, allow the Spirit of God to influence and impact everything in your life – your mind (everything you think), your will (every action you do), and your emotions (everything you feel). "Be filled" is also a **present** tense **passive** voice command just like the command to "not be drunk with wine." The idea communicated is NOT only an urgency to fulfill this command, but a desire that this would be something we would continually fulfill. This is not something husbands should check into for one hour on Sunday morning and then check out of for the rest of the week. This is not something husbands should check into a moment before they open their Bibles for Bible study and then check out of the second they close their Bibles. This is to be taken seriously as something that needs urgent and ongoing attention. Also, because it is a **passive** command, the idea communicated is that this is something that happens TO the believer and is NOT something done BY the believer. In other words, right now, begin allowing yourself to be filled by the Spirit of God in a consistent and ongoing manner. Dr. Tom Constable states in his notes on Ephesians 5:18 that another way to translated this command is: "Be being kept filled by the Spirit."[94] So, the believer is to allow, through active faith and reliance upon, the Spirit of God to act upon the believer in filling him or her with something, but what is it?

---

[94] Tom Constable, "Notes on Ephesians," *Plano Bible Chapel*, last modified 2020, accessed November 17, 2020, https://www.planobiblechapel.org/tcon/notes/html/nt/ephesians/ephesians.htm.

Looking at the verse closer, one notices the word translated "with," which is the Greek preposition **en**, which can also be translated "by." In fact, the essence of the word "by" seems to fit better with this context describing what Paul is commanding here. He seems to be commanding the allowance of the Spirit of God to be the agent of filling, filling the believer with the life of Jesus Christ. Picture a pitcher of water, filling a cup. The pitcher pictures the Holy Spirit, the water pictures the Lord Jesus Christ, and the cup pictures the believer. This concept of the Holy Spirit as the agent of filling and the life of the Lord Jesus as the content of the filling also seems to be corroborated by other Bible passages, such as Galatians 2:20 – "I have been crucified with Christ; it is no longer I who live, **but Christ lives in me**; and the *life* which I now live in the flesh I live by faith in the Son of God, who loved me and gave Himself for me," Colossians 1:29 – "To them God willed to make known what are the riches of the glory of this mystery among the Gentiles: **which is Christ in you**, the hope of glory," 2 Corinthians 3:18 – "But we all, with unveiled face, beholding as in a mirror the glory of the Lord, **are being transformed into the same image from glory to glory, just as by the Spirit of the Lord**," and 2

Corinthians 4:10-11 – "Always carrying about in the body the dying of the Lord Jesus, that the life of Jesus also may be manifested in our body. For we who live are always delivered to death for Jesus' sake, that the life of Jesus also may be manifested in our mortal flesh." Men, does Jesus Christ know how to love your wife? Yes, He knows exactly what she needs – He knows the words she needs, and He knows when she needs silence. He knows the physical touch or comfort she needs, and He knows when she does not want to be touched. He knows when to solve her problems, and He knows when to simply listen to her vent. Jesus knows all these things, so instead of trying to figure all of this out as a husband, why NOT "be filled by the Spirit" with the life of Christ and depend upon the Lord and His resources to execute this command to "love your wife?"

Being filled with the Spirit of God is the KEY to all of the relational injunctions described in the verses that follow (Ephesians 5:22-6:9). To be a biblical husband, you must "be filled by the Spirit," to be a biblical wife, you must "be filled by the Spirit," to be a good son, daughter, father, mother, employer, employee, etc., you must also "be filled by the Spirit." Just as wine controls and influences everything in your life (your speech, your actions, your thinking, etc.), now allow the Spirit of God to do the same. If I told husbands that today I could let Jesus Christ into their homes to minister to their wives, that He would be there to encourage her, build her up, and listen to her and respond to her in areas in which they are frustrated with her, I think they would all gladly move aside and let Him come inside. In fact, if it cost money to rent Jesus for the day, just to do this for their wives, many men would NOT hesitate to pay any asking price. This is the point though – Christian husbands already have access to Christ's very life! They must learn to walk by means of the Spirit to access those resources. What wives need more than another bouquet of flowers or another box of chocolates is for their husbands to be convinced and fully persuaded that they MUST be filled by the Spirit more consistently in order to love their wives.

Too many sincere Christian men are trying to love their wives in their own strength, and that is why they absolutely **STINK** at it! These men are inconsistent, they fluctuate back and forth from being willing one day to sacrifice for their wives to being unwilling the very next day to sacrifice for them. These men point fingers at their wives' inconsistencies and use those as an excuse to shirk away from their own responsibilities. These men and their love for their wives are dependent upon certain circumstances and on certain responses from their wives, and hence nothing in their approach is stable or consistent! What we are going to see in this passage (Ephesians 5:25-33) is it does not matter what is going on with the other side (with the wife); it only matters what is going on internally between the husband and the Lord Jesus. This is the husband living life as unto the Lord regardless of if, how, when, or what type of response comes back from his wife. Many people say that marriage is 50-50, and the husband has to do his part, and the wife has to do her part. I understand their sentiment, and where they are going, but when it comes to the husband and wife fulfilling their God-given and God-ordained role, it is not 50-50. To say that it is 50-50 means that the fulfillment of the husband's role is in some way contingent upon the wife's response and vice versa. Understanding this distinction can be revolutionary for some husbands, whose love has always been conditional. Culture teaches conditional love, whereas the word of God teaches unconditional love that is impossible to execute without the empowering work of the Holy Spirit.

So, for husbands, in verse 25, we have one of the weightiest commands in all of Scripture: "Husbands, love your wives, just as Christ also loved the church and gave Himself for her." It is weighty because we need to find and utilize the proper resources to execute this command. Just running off and "doing it" (a la Nike) is going to be much like trying to cut a lawn with a scalpel! Before diving into the text, Dr. Harold Hoehner, in his commentary on Ephesians, makes an excellent cultural comment here when he writes, "This exhortation to husbands to love their wives is unique. It is not found in the Old Testament, rabbinic literature, or in the household codes of the Greco-Roman era. Although the hierarchical model of the home is maintained, it is ameliorated by this revolutionary exhortation that husbands are to love their wives as Christ loved the church."[95] It is interesting that our culture takes issue with verse 22 and loves verse 25. In Paul's culture, verse 22 did not even raise an eyebrow, and yet verse 25 flipped most people's worlds upside down! For a husband to love his wife

---

[95] Harold W. Hoehner, Ephesians: An Exegetical Commentary, (Grand Rapids: Baker Academic, 2002), 748.

in a self-sacrificial way was so contrary to the culture and so contrary to human nature really!

The command "love your wives" is a **present** tense command, indicating immediate and urgent action is required, and it is in the **active** voice, meaning that the husband must choose to engage in this action. This action will involve his active, ongoing volition to do so. This does not say, "Love her once she starts submitting more consistently," nor does it say, "Love her once she apologizes to you," and nor does it say, "Love her when she cleans up her act." This type of love is NOT a one-time declaration but a moment-by-moment exhibition over the course of one's lifetime. One of the things we see about the word "love" that Paul uses is that it is the word **agapao**, which is used six times in this passage. Generally, the word **agapao** or **agape** (noun form) is used to describe the type of love that seeks the highest good for another person. As one commentator has described it, it is the "all give" type of love. It is interesting that Paul does NOT choose the Greek word, **eros**, reflecting sexual love or **phileo**, which reflects friendship love. No, Paul uses the word for "love" that he also uses in 1 Corinthians 13. In addition, he uses the word for "love" that describes what the Spirit of God produces in the believer (the fruit of the Spirit) in Galatians 5:22-23. As an illustration, take a test. Determine for the next 30 days to love your wife no matter what and really put your head down and do it. Guess what is going to happen on day 31? You are going to feel unappreciated. You are going to think, "Man, she has not really even thanked me for this. I gave her the best month of her life, and she is not even appreciative!" At this moment, you just switched tracks in your thinking – the previous 30 days were "love at whatever cost," and now it is "love with contingencies." So, if we are being honest, the husband should have ONE and ONLY ONE reaction to this command: **sheer terror and fear** due to his recognition of his own inadequacy to do it!

Husbands need not follow the example of the Israelites when confronted by the word of the Lord in Exodus 19:7-8 when Moses "laid before them all these words which the Lord commanded him," to which the people replied, "All that the Lord has spoken we will do." What an immature and foolish response! What a lack of recognition of one's own weakness and inadequacy to fulfill his or her own commitment. Husbands are in the same exact scenario when it comes to fulfilling this command. In fact, most husbands are both foolish and immature enough to believe that they can just DO it, just like they have DONE school, like they have DONE work, like they have DONE their career, like they have DONE fixing cars, and like they have DONE playing sports. In other words, they feel like they can just **WILL** their way to success. However, loving one's wife does not work this way! In fact, when husbands do fail in loving their wives, it is often observed that they just **TRY** harder! If you want to guarantee ongoing and future failure in your marriage, just **TRY** harder to be a better husband. You'll ensure guaranteed failure to love your wife as Christ loved the Church! Do not try to do what no man on earth has ever been able to do or figure out. Do not try to love your wife without the resources of God's grace. Husbands need to realize that it is NOT about trying harder but about trusting in the Lord more consistently! It is crucial for husbands, when they come to this command, to understand that deliverance and success as a husband is not to be occupied with how to be a better husband, but rather it is to learn how to more consistently occupy yourself with Jesus Christ.

Now, Paul goes on in verse 25 to provide a practical example or comparison for husbands as to HOW it should look. He says, "just as Christ…" Christ is the example! You talk about raising the bar even higher! The bar is NOT even in view anymore; it has been raised so high! Throw away your W.W.J.D. bracelets because this is NOT what Paul is talking about at all here. It is NOT about imitating Jesus Christ; it is about His life being lived out in and through us. At this standard, husbands should be crying "UNCLE" at this point! The depth of their own inadequacy as husbands should be setting in!

The first comparison that Paul uses to "flesh out" the example, or the standard, of Jesus Christ is that Christ "loved" (**agapao**) the Church. We know from the Word of God that Jesus Christ loves her on the basis of **grace**, meaning the Church did not deserve it, nor will she ever deserve it. This is exactly how Adam originally accepted and loved Eve before the fall. Unfortunately, this is the opposite of how husbands typically love their wives. Many husbands wait for their wives to merit their love, they wait for them to earn or deserve their love, and they will even give her the silent treatment, waiting to get that response that they feel they are entitled to before they cut loose any love. In contrast, how did Christ love practically? Well, Christ's love is **unchangeable** and **cannot be broken** (Romans 8:35-39). It is not based on the behavior of the Church; otherwise, grace is not grace and agape love is not agape love! We know that Christ **prayed** for believers and **continually prays** for them (John 17:20-26 and Romans 8:34). We know that Christ **reveals** Himself and His plan to the Church (Ephesians 3:3-5 and Colossians 1:26-27). In other words, He is transparent and engaged in His communication with her. We also know that Christ provides **rest** and bears the load in life (Matthew 11:28-30).

The second comparison that Paul uses to "flesh out" the example, or the standard, of Jesus Christ is that Jesus Christ "gave Himself" **FOR** the Church. In fact, Christ demonstrated this love through laying down His own life (Romans 5:8). He kept NOTHING back for her, He did not self-protect. He sacrificed everything with her in mind. Now, apply that to husbands and their wives. This means that the penalty for **EVERY** mistake by the Church, intentional or not, and **EVERY** rejection of Jesus Christ by the Church, intentional or not, was paid in full by Jesus Christ. This means that the Church has never and will never have to pay for her own sins. The mindset of Adam, immediately following the fall, and the mindset of every carnal man is simply the opposite: "I do not want to sacrifice for her! She should get what she deserves!" By pointing the finger at Eve, Adam was basically telling the Lord, "Go ahead and execute the death penalty on Eve, Lord! Just spare me please!" This is the opposite of the sacrifice of Jesus Christ – this is cowardly! In many Christian marriages, the husband is making sure that his wife pays for her sins, and he does this in a variety of different ways: the silent treatment, not listening to her, not engaging with her or sharing his thoughts or feelings, withholding personal touch, etc. Imagine if Jesus Christ loved us in that manner – He would have given up on many of us years ago. Because Jesus is the example given, the effect of the command is that husbands need to give of themselves <u>sacrificially</u> despite how they feel, how their wives are treating them, how things are going at work, and how any other circumstances in their life are going. Husbands, our wives NEVER deserve to receive the brunt of our frustrations with life, circumstances, trials, etc. Husbands have divine resources at their disposal and must become better adept at utilizing them more consistently, so they can live up to this impossible standard. To

LOVE one's wife "just as" Christ loved the Church is truly an impossible standard made ONLY possible with grace resources!

Now, Paul is going to give two purposes or two reasons why Jesus Christ loved the Church in the two aforementioned ways. These purposes or results are indicated by the word translated "that" (**hina**) in verses 26 and 27. The first purpose or result of Christ's love is found in verse 26 — "that He might sanctify and cleanse her with the washing of water by the word." One of the keys to understanding this passage is to stay really "tight" with the example of Jesus Christ and then build backwards to what it should look like in the husband. To "sanctify" meant to make holy or to set apart from a common use to a sacred or special use.[96] Hold this definition in your mind because when we work backwards to make application to the husband, it will be helpful. So, to say that Christ sanctified the church means that the moment a person puts his or her faith in Jesus Christ, he or she is positionally sanctified and set apart by the Spirit of God into the body of Christ (1 Corinthians 12:13). 1 Corinthians 1:30 also says, "But of Him you

---

[96] Zodhiates, The Complete Word Study Dictionary, 37.

are in Christ Jesus, who became for us wisdom from God—and righteousness and sanctification and redemption." God is the One who set us apart IN Christ Jesus, and it was accomplished via His finished work for us (when He gave Himself for us), and it is manifested in our lives when we put our faith in Jesus Christ. Basically, before salvation, we were in a position of destruction (i.e., in Adam), and, when we believed, we were set apart into a special place designed for a special use. It is in this privileged position that we have been blessed with every spiritual blessing in the heavenly places, according to Ephesians 1:3.

So, what is the connection to HOW husbands should love their wives? In the same way, husbands give of themselves sacrificially to set their wives in a place of special value rather than viewing their wives as "common." The mindset of the husband should be that his wife is "set apart" in a special place and position in his thinking, his priorities, and his efforts. J. Hampton Keathley IV adds, "They (wives) are set apart for special protection, special care, for special attention, for a special purpose. You have taken her out of the world and set her apart because you want to devote special attention to her."[97] By marrying your wife, husband, you have taken her out of the world and have set her apart in a special position of being your wife – ONLY yours, and your wife, and her ONLY, deserves your complete and undivided attention and priority.

Now, let's quickly go back to Jesus Christ and how He sanctified the Church because this will give us even further insight into applying this to husbands. Jesus Christ sanctified the Church **by OR through** "cleaning her with the washing of the water by the spoken word." The word translated "cleanse" is a participle explaining HOW the sanctifying work is effected.[98] So, in this case, the sanctifying work, this cleansing, is accomplished through the spoken word (**rhema**). By definition, **rhema** is something definitely or expressly stated. It could be an official announcement or even a treaty, but the predominant idea is something communicated.[99] It is interesting to note that the word **logos** is **NOT** used here, which speaks

---

[97] Keathley, "Loving Your Wife."
[98] "Cleanse" is an aorist participle (constative also) and describes HOW the sanctifying is effected: 'That He might sanctify it, by cleansing…' – Homer A. Kent, Jr., Ephesians: The Glory of the Church, (Chicago: Moody Publishers, 1971), 102.
[99] Zodhiates, The Complete Word Study Dictionary, 4487.

more to the written word! Now, this should not surprise us regarding Jesus Christ, who through His spoken word, spoke light into existence. In this case, it was His spoken word that set the Church apart. Additionally, this cleansing from filth is related to regeneration and the new birth (Titus 3:5), and this was ultimately accomplished, so that believers were free to become something new. So, where and how does this apply to husbands? In the same way, the words that husbands use can assist in communicating to their wives' their place of special value and importance. This type of verbal communication encourages their wives and allows them to bloom and flourish where they are. This verbal communication is what continues to "set apart their wives" in a special place of unique privilege and worth in their eyes. One such way husbands can do this, which is very practical and very biblical, is to remind their wives of their glorious position IN Christ — the worth and value that they possess in God's eyes, how God has a plan and purpose for them in spite of their self-perceived imperfections, etc. Husbands, your wives are having their value and worth chipped away at every turn! They go to the grocery store, and they see nothing but airbrushed models telling them that they are not pretty enough. They go to work, and they face all sorts of criticism about their work, not being a good Mom, not being the best employee, etc. They go to church, and they are not accepted there because there are social groups and cliques already formed. Wives need to hear from their husbands their inestimable value and worth to Jesus Christ, because with a cacophony of other voices, the husbands' voices need to be the loudest and most distinct. Husbands can learn this very practical way to "love their wives as Christ loved the Church."

Furthermore, the second purpose or result of Christ loving and giving of Himself for the Church is found in verse 27: "that He might present her to Himself a glorious Church." To "present" means to stand near or before someone.[100] In this case, the Lord is causing the Church to stand near or before Him. This is amazing! Jesus Christ is presenting His Church to Himself! In other words, His care and love for the Church is personal and constant. You know what is so interesting about this is when you think of human weddings, does the husband go down into the bridal room and do

---

[100] Zodhiates, The Complete Word Study Dictionary, 3936.

his bride's hair? Does he do her makeup? No, he does not get her ready for her presentation at the wedding; she does it all, and she presents herself to her groom at the end of the walkway. This distinction is KEY to notice. Whereas human brides prepare themselves for their husbands, Christ prepares His own bride for Himself. Jesus Christ is personally attending to His bride, and He will ensure her successful presentation in her glorification! Jesus' bride is described as a "glorious" Church, defined as not having spot or wrinkle or any such thing, being holy and blameless. We know that this presentation is based solely upon His work **FOR** her! Christ shielded the Church from the punishment she deserved and stood in her stead.

So, what is the connection to HOW husbands should love their wives? Well, we know Adam did the exact opposite! He threw Eve under the bus and blamed her for everything. Adam probably did not know exactly what "death" was, but he decided she should get it, not himself. Husbands, when walking according to the flesh, will do the same thing. Husbands will blame their wives for everything, and they almost will communicate the foolish notion that if it were not for their wives, they themselves would be perfect.

They would never sin! They would never lose their temper! This is what carnality produces – a self-aggrandizing view of oneself! In going back to Christ's example, notice that Christ takes the responsibility for His bride's presentation and successful examination. Husbands, too, are to stand beside their wives, shielding them, building them up, and bearing some of the load incurred from their own faults. They should follow Christ's example of what a Spirit-filled husband should look like. In fact, one of the things we are going to see develop further here is that husbands should build their wives up in such a way that God's purposes can be fulfilled in her. Trust me, men, when you can function in this way as a husband, only desiring God's purposes to be fulfilled in your wives' lives and walking by faith to love your wives as Christ loved the Church, you can experience Heaven on earth. However, the exact opposite often happens and many men blame their wives for this failure when they themselves are the ones contributing to this overall mess. Husbands must understand and be convinced that one KEY mechanism that God uses in their wives' spiritual growth is their own love for them, and THIS (Christ's example) is what "loving" and "sacrificial" husbands look like.

Now, as we move onto verses 28-32, we need to understand that Paul applies the truths given in verses 25–27. Also, the overarching theme or concept of these verses is the truth shared in verse 31 – husband and wives, in God's estimation, are ONE FLESH. Now, for many, this truth seems really simple and very basic. It's kind of like, "Tell me something I don't know, right? I mean I read this all the way back in Genesis!" However, this truth should impact the husband's mindset in all his dealings and interactions with his wife. This is a KEY point that the Lord is bringing together for us through the apostle Paul because He is providing us with divine perspective on marriage. So, verse 28 says, "So husbands ought to love their own wives as their own bodies; he who loves his wife loves himself." The word "so" here refers to what precedes, and, in this case, Paul is referring to HOW Christ loves the Church because the Church is His own body! They "ought" to, meaning husbands are indebted to love their wives in the way described. This is God's design for marriage and His solution for wedded bliss, so husbands should take a biblical stance in their thinking. Paul uses this example because implied is that husbands naturally love their own bodies in this "all-give" and "unconditional" way, but husbands are to begin taking this biblical stance, this divine viewpoint. Husbands' wives are part of themselves – they are one flesh! The point is this. If husbands are hungry, they get themselves food to eat. If husbands are thirsty, they get themselves something to drink. If husbands are tired, they get into bed and get some sleep. If husbands are upset, they turn to things that provide them comfort. Basically, if husbands have needs, they do everything in their own power to meet those needs — naturally. In the same way, husbands are to view the needs of their wives and desire to meet them, whether those needs are physical, emotional, verbal, non-verbal, time-oriented, spiritual, financial, etc. Why? Because their wives are part of them – they are ONE FLESH. This is the argument Paul is putting forward here. Now, in order to do this, the husband must: (1) Know that this is essential for him fulfilling his role, (2) Take a proactive interest in his wife – NEVER stop studying her, and (3) Rely upon the Spirit of God (5:18) to be consistent with this. Just having the right desires is not enough to execute those desires and thus relying upon the Spirit of God to produce the life of Jesus Christ in us becomes so essential in providing the power to execute these right desires.

Paul goes on to say, "He who loves his wife loves himself." Notice, the self-related benefit that a husband gets when he loves his wife as Christ loves the Church – He truly loves himself and even the care for him and his life will flourish! This loving is a present tense verb with ongoing emphasis. In other words, if the husband loves his wife biblically, he will benefit from it in his own daily life. Paul is going to go on to say that if you really believe the biblical doctrine that, at marriage, you and your wife become one flesh, then you will understand that if you love your wife biblically, you will also take care of yourself because you are ONE FLESH!

In fact, this ONE FLESH emphasis keeps coming up in this section as verse 29 reads, "For no one ever hated his own flesh, but nourishes and cherishes it, just as the Lord does the church." The word "for" expands upon this thought of husbands loving their wives as themselves, and Paul uses very exclusive language here — NO ONE "hates" his or her own flesh, meaning to take an active ill will in words and/or conduct towards someone! NO ONE does this! In fact, Paul says there are two ways that we approach caring for ourselves, and these are undisputed facts. The first fact is that husbands **NOURISH** themselves. The word translated "nourishes" is a compound word in the Greek (**ektrepho**) with the preposition "ek," giving an emphatic emphasis to the root word, meaning to nourish, to rear, in terms of child-rearing, or to feed someone (See Matthew 6:26 where it is used of how God "feeds" the birds). Because this is a present indicative, it indicates ongoing and non-stop care of our own bodies in terms of raising or nourishing with food.

The second fact Paul gives is that husbands **CHERISH** themselves. The word translated "cherishes" means to make warm or to heat. The word is used elsewhere in the Scriptures to describe how a nursing mother takes care of her children (See 1 Thessalonians 2:7). This verb is also a present indicative, and thus it indicates ongoing and non-stop care of our own bodies in terms of shelter, provision, and safety. Now, Paul brings up a subtle, yet significant, third indisputable fact. This fact comes by way of example and comparison, and yet there is an incredibly subtle *SWITCH* in Paul's analogy! Notice that husbands nourish and cherish themselves **JUST AS** Christ does the Church. Notice that the analogy veers off the expected course, and it **DOES NOT** SAY "just as Christ does Himself!" Jesus nourishes and cherishes the Church as naturally as husbands nourish and cherish themselves. Hence, this brings into sharp focus WHY husbands need to be filled with the Spirit. Jesus does NOT need to be convinced to love the Church – He does! Jesus does NOT need to be pleaded with to care for the Church – He does! Jesus naturally does this, and, as husbands walk by means of the Spirit, they, too, can love and care for their wives the way Jesus naturally does the Church. The reason for this is that Jesus Christ understands the union between Himself and His body of believers. The husband must take the mindset of the Lord Jesus. One of the things that biblical love does is it motivates proper response. This is why 2 Corinthians 5:14 says, "For the love of Christ compels us, because we judge thus: that if One died for all, then all died." Love is a proper motivator, and Jesus knows that His loving care of the Church is the best way to achieve consistent, stable, and long-lasting growth in the Church. The same can be true of a loving husband. He can be a tool in the hand of God to motivate, encourage, and spur on spiritual growth in his wife.

Verses 30-32 go on to make some conclusions regarding this ONE FLESH relationship and mindset — "For we are members of His body, of His flesh and of His bones. For this reason, a man shall leave his father and mother and be joined to his wife, and the two shall become one flesh. This is a great mystery, but I speak concerning Christ and the church." The word "for" gives us further explanation as to WHY Jesus nourishes and cherishes the Church. Again, because Jesus understands that the Church is ONE with Him, husbands should also recognize that their wives are ONE with themselves. So, in order for the husband to experience the full divine enjoyment of marriage, he must take the mind of the Lord Jesus. Jesus recognizes that this approach is the best way to achieve consistent, stable, and long-lasting growth and a properly motivated response. Husbands, do you want a DREAM wife? Be a DREAM husband, filled by the Spirit of God, allowing the Lord to accomplish this THROUGH you! Marriage will never be more fulfilling than this!

Now, the "mystery" spoken of in verse 32 is that Christ's union with the Church is the exact same type of union between husband and wife (i.e., ONE flesh). It is this union that guarantees every blessing you possess and every promise that God will keep. It is interesting because the "mystery" here is NOT that husband and wife become ONE FLESH at marriage. That was revealed in Genesis 2:24, which says, "Therefore a man shall leave his father and mother and be joined to his wife, and they shall become one flesh." What was NOT revealed in the Old Testament and thus categorized as a "mystery" is that Christ and His Church would be ONE FLESH. The Old Testament predicted Emmanuel, God with us, but never in a million years would anyone have understood that the Messiah would be in a ONE FLESH (believers IN Him, **AND** He IN believers) relationship with His Church! As a believer, our union with Christ is the most unique and special bond of connection that has ever existed in the world, and it was **NOT** known or revealed before the Church-age.

Wow! What a high calling and privilege it is to be a husband! God is calling husbands to a higher plane that can only be reached only by utilizing the resources God provides. May husbands be convinced of two things: (1) The day they marry their wives they are no longer two individuals, but ONE FLESH. Everything they do to benefit and love them will benefit themselves, and (2) The only way to consistently love their wives "just as" Christ loved the Church is to walk by faith, so that Jesus Christ can love their wives through their mortal bodies. As 2 Corinthians 4:10-11 says, "Always carrying about in the body the dying of the Lord Jesus, **that the** life of Jesus also may be manifested in our body.** For we who live are always delivered to death for Jesus' sake, **that the life of Jesus also may be manifested in our mortal flesh."

CHAPTER 8
HOW TO BE A BIBLICAL HUSBAND PART 2

Additional Scriptures contribute to our understanding of what a biblical husband looks like. It cannot be emphasized enough that it is NOT in trying to become a better husband that a man becomes a biblical husband. It is when that man, cognizant of his own lack of resources to love his wife in a biblical way, begins to trust in the Lord and be filled by His Spirit that he will begin to function biblically as a husband. This can happen in the first year of marriage, even on the first day! It can also happen as a believing husband, who has walked carnally for years, realizes his need for God's grace resources and begins in that moment to rely upon the Spirit of God to produce the life of Christ in and through him.

Colossians 3:19 is a similar verse to Ephesians 5:25, and yet we pick up an additional "subtle" distinction. Colossians 3:19 says, "Husbands, love your wives and do not be bitter toward them." The similarities between this passage and the passage in Ephesians 5 are readily observed. In Colossians 3:16-18, we a similar pattern as Ephesians 5:18-21. The result of being "filled by the Spirit" in Ephesians 5:18 is the following: (1) speaking to one another in psalms and hymns and spiritual songs, (2) singing and making melody in your heart to the Lord, (3) giving thanks, and (4) submitting to one another. The result of "letting the Word of Christ dwell in your richly" in Colossians 3:16 is the following: (1) teaching and admonishing one another in psalms and hymns and spiritual songs, (2) singing with grace in your hearts, (3) doing and saying all everything in Jesus' name, and (4) giving thanks. Thus, in this sense, the instruction of Colossians 3:19 also assumes divine resources at the husband's disposal.

This is why the command is the same – "Love your wives!" In fact, Paul uses the same exact Greek word **agapao** and the same exact grammatical form (present, active imperative) as the verb in Ephesians 5:25. Now, contextually this makes sense as Paul wrote both Ephesians and Colossians at roughly the same time during his Roman imprisonment, but, Paul adds an additional command in Colossians 3:19 that he did not include in the entirety of the Ephesians 5 passage – "Do not be bitter toward them (your wives)." Whereas the repeated command from Ephesians is more positive (you should do *THIS*), this is the first hint of something you "should **NOT** do" as a husband. The very fact that Paul teaches husbands

NOT to do this indicates that husbands probably have an easy time sliding into this mode and, thus, need to be corrected and warned. The word translated "be bitter" means to make bitter or to embitter.[101] The original root meaning of the word communicates the idea of something that is "pointed" OR "sharp" (like arrows), something that is "penetrating" (like a smell), something that is "painful" (to the feelings), OR something that is "bitter" (to the taste).[102] It is helpful to note here what the typical response is when all or any of these aforementioned things happen – we pull back! If something is sharp or pokey, we pull back. If we smell something putrid, we pull back and move away from it. If somebody hurts our feelings, we generally pull back so as not to be continually hurt. If we taste something bitter, our natural response is to recoil in disgust, and we pull back from what we are eating. Thus, the thrust of this word, in terms of how a husband SHOULD NOT respond, is to not allow yourself to get to a point where you are pulling away from your wife.

---

[101] Zodhiates, The Complete Word Study Dictionary, 4087.
[102] Kittel, Gerhard ; Friedrich, Gerhard ; Bromiley, Geoffrey William: *Theological Dictionary of the New Testament*. Grand Rapids, Mich. : W.B. Eerdmans, 1995, c1985, S. 839

This concept is brought out further, as we look at this command more closely. It is interesting to note something that is unique about this command — it is in the **passive voice**. Thus, the idea communicated here is to not allow yourself to become embittered or to behave harshly toward your wife. In other words, what is ironic about this command is that this is not something the husband is "actively" pursuing, but rather it is something that is "acting" on him. In fact, many times, he may not even know it is happening, but this type of response could set in over time. This type of bitterness can sneak up on a husband who is NOT pursuing consistent fellowship with the Lord. It could be little things that irritate him about his wife which continue to build up and build up to the point where he has no desire to even be near her anymore. Maybe she has slighted him in a conversation with friends, maybe she did not do something that he expected her to do, maybe she did not say something in his defense that he expected her to say, maybe she asked one too many times about when he was going to fix her vacuum cleaner, maybe, she does not understand or care about the stress he is under at work. We could go on and on! At some point, these types of things have built up, and he has allowed himself to become embittered toward her. Once husbands get to this point, BOOM! She is the enemy, she is the problem, she is the issue, and she is now the brunt of his frustration. Unfortunately, she has no idea what has been cooking under the surface, so she says, "Hey, when you get a chance could you put the trash out?" By the way, that's a very reasonable request, but that is when the husband explodes on her! His response and reaction do NOT meet the request, which is when you know that something has been cooking under the surface. The husband has just violated what Paul is teaching here, as he started entertaining thoughts from the sin nature, thoughts like the following: "I have got rights," "How dare she mistreat me," and "How dare she disrespect me." Hence, instead of the husband recognizing these thoughts are springing from the sin nature and (by faith) counting upon his co-crucifixion and co-resurrection with Christ to free him from sin's power, he starts to swirl these thoughts around in his thinking. These thoughts become what husbands occupy themselves with, and, before long, bitterness acts on them, and it begins to control them. They then either implode, which happens for a lot of people, or they explode. Typically, wives receive the brunt of it, and then they are like, "Wow! I'll never ask him to take out the trash again!" However, it really had nothing to do with the trash and everything to do with the way the husband, who has all the resources he needs in Christ, would not respond to carnal thoughts by trusting in the Lord's method for delivering him from sin's power. So, husbands must understand that this is something that is an ever-lurking potential danger in their marriage. Bitterness, in general, is contrary to love and emanates from the sin nature! Hebrews 12:15 says, "Looking carefully lest anyone fall short of the grace of God; lest any root of bitterness springing up cause trouble, and by this many become defiled." When we do NOT take advantage of our grace resources in Jesus Christ, bitterness can spring up within us without us even suspecting it, and this can cause great damage in our marriage.

Another verse that sheds additional light on the role of a husband is found in 1 Peter 3:7, which says, "Husbands, likewise, dwell with them with understanding, giving honor to the wife, as to the weaker vessel, and as being heirs together of the grace of life, that your prayers may not be hindered." The word "likewise" gives us an indicator that we must look further up in the context to see what Peter is referencing. However, as we go back up to verse 1, where Peter addresses the wives' role in marriage, he also uses a "likewise" so we are forced to go back into chapter 2 to find out what Peter is saying for the husbands to do likewise. Going back to 1 Peter 2:21-25, one can see that the main principle taught there is committing OR entrusting judgment of oneself to God. In fact, this conclusion is based upon the way Jesus Christ did this very thing in His own life when He suffered unjustly. The word "commit," as translated in 2:23, means to deliver over or up to the power of someone else.[103] In other words, Jesus did NOT try to deliver Himself, did NOT try to enforce justice on those mistreating Him, and did NOT try to control everything, so He got the best circumstantial outcome. Jesus Christ merely trusted His well-being, His life, and His mistreatment by others to God the Father, Whom He knew would handle things the right and good way. This same attitude is the one that husbands must bring into marriage. As it has been said before, husbands need to leave the "self-preservation at all costs" attitude OUT of their marriages!

---

[103] Zodhiates, The Complete Word Study Dictionary, 3860.

This "likewise" sets the stage for the instruction found in this verse. The first instruction is for husbands to "dwell with them (their wives) with understanding." So, in the same way Jesus entrusted His life and well-being to the Lord, husbands are to reside with their wives, NOT protecting themselves but attempting to live with their wives in an understanding way. The word Paul uses here for "understanding" represents a present, fragmentary knowledge (**gnosis**) in contrast to the word, which means full and complete knowledge (**epignosis**). As Dr. Charles Swindoll put it, "This doesn't refer to an academic knowledge of her, but to a deep understanding of how she is put together. It involves perceiving her innermost make-up, discerning her deep-seated concerns and fears, and helping her work through them in the safety and security of your love."[104] It has been rightly said that this is not an exhortation to "understand" our wives, which is impossible, but rather an encouragement to live with them in an understanding way. Dr. Warren Wiersbe puts it this way, "A Christian

---

[104] Charles R. Swindoll, Hope in Hurtful Times: A Study of 1 Peter, (Anaheim, CA.: Insight for Living, 1990), 57-58.

husband needs to know his wife's moods, feelings, needs, fears, and hopes. He needs to 'listen with his heart' and share meaningful communication with her. There must be in the home such a protective atmosphere of love and submission that the husband and wife can disagree and still be happy together."[105] I am going to write down something that everyone knows — women are different than men. I think all husbands have made that realization, but the point of this verse is NOT to criticize our wives for being different but to recognize and embrace their differences and understand that they will not see everything the same way. This is okay in a marriage, and, quite frankly, it is a blessing, and husbands must begin to see it in this way, too. Just because a wife sees something differently than her husband or just because she reacts differently than him to different circumstantial stimuli does not make her wrong, **NOR** should it threaten the husband's security or safety as the leader of the home. Husbands are to live with an intelligent recognition of the nature of the marriage relationship

---

[105] Warren W. Wiersbe, Be Hopeful: How to Make the Best of Times Out of Your Worst of Times, (Colorado Springs: Chariot Victor Publishing, 1982), 74.

regarding their wives' makeup and wiring, and they are NOT to actively try to change the wiring of their wives as if something is wrong with them. In other words, you attempt to adjust to her and NOT expect her to adjust to you in everything in your lives. So, in essence, husbands need to be students of their wives. They have a subject they can study for the rest of their lives — their wives! This will require active listening to the wife as well as the study of her temperament, emotions, personality, and thought patterns. Husbands have only one lifelong subject, and there will even be pop quizzes along the way! Dr. Thomas Constable puts it in a very practical way when he writes, "One of a husband's primary responsibilities in a marriage is caring for his wife. Caring requires understanding. If you are married, what are your wife's greatest needs? Ask her. What are her greatest concerns? Ask her. What are her hopes and dreams? Ask her. What new vistas would she like to explore? Ask her and keep on asking her over the years! Her answers will enable you to understand and to care for her more effectively."[106] It is a tall order to know one's wife, to understand her, even to be understanding with her. Again, it can only be done when husbands are walking by means of the Spirit.

The second instruction that Peter provides is just as significant when he writes that husbands, likewise, need to be "giving honor to the wife." The word translated "giving" means to allot, assign, apportion, or to bestow.[107] Additionally, the word used with "giving," translated "honor" means dignity, honor, respect, reverence or value.[108] When you put the two together, you have the idea of bestowing or assigning high value to something or someone. This same word ("honor") is used to describe the proceeds gained in the sale of land (Acts 5:2) and the honorable position that Aaron held as the High Priest of Israel (Hebrews 5:4). Thus, in this context, the husband is instructed to place a "high value" upon his wife. **AGAIN**, as was emphasized in Ephesians 5, if a husband believes that his

---

[106] Tom Constable, "Notes on 1 Peter," *Plano Bible Chapel*, last modified 2020, accessed November 17, 2020, https://www.planobiblechapel.org/tcon/notes/html/nt/1peter/1peter.htm.
[107] Zodhiates, The Complete Word Study Dictionary, 632.
[108] Zodhiates, The Complete Word Study Dictionary, 5092.

wife has high value, and he treats her accordingly, HE will personally reap the benefit of it because they are one flesh! Wiersbe writes, "The husband must be the 'thermostat' in the home, setting the emotional and spiritual temperature. The wife often is the 'thermometer,' letting him know what the temperature is!"[109]

Peter goes on to provide another subtle description that is so helpful for husbands in understanding HOW to give honor or high value to their wives "as to the weaker vessel." Now, some women might take offense to this statement, but this description is very helpful when we understand the imagery Peter is using. He describes women as the "weaker vessel" just in terms of physicality. They are NOT inferior in any way! So, the idea communicated is that husbands place high value on their wives by dealing with them more delicately and with great care. It is different than a husband would treat his buddies. Dr. Thomas Constable artfully writes, "Both the husband and the wife are vessels, but husbands are more typically similar to iron skillets whereas wives resemble china vases, being more

---

[109] Wiersbe, Be Hopeful, 75.

delicate. They are equally important but different."[110] Like in Ephesians, wives should be set apart in their husbands' thinking as one who is special and worthy of unique care and attention. Peter goes on to say that a negative consequence for not treating one's wife in the manner prescribed is "that your prayers may not be hindered." Not only does this reflect a disruption of fellowship between the husband and God, but this also means that the prayers of an inattentive husband could be "cut off" or "fruitless."

So, in summary for the husband, note the following: (1) love your wife just as Christ loved the Church, (2) do not be embittered against your wife, and (3) live with your wife in an understanding way. Again, as one final reminder and exhortation to the husbands, husbands cannot do this effectively or consistently if they are not walking by means of the Spirit. Husbands, you need to be spiritual to obey. You need to be spiritual to execute your divine role and divinely-given duties!

---

[110] Constable, "Notes on 1 Peter."

CHAPTER 9
HOW TO BE A BIBLICAL WIFE PART 1

The introduction to chapter 7, regarding the biblical role of a husband, could simply be cut and pasted into this chapter as well. Every successful team in the history of the world is comprised of individual people, performing his or her individual roles, and the team experiences success. Marriage is NO different! On this team, both husband and wife have his or her individual roles and duties, each of which must be fulfilled in order for true marital success.

I am reminded of a story from the sports world that illustrates the concept of NOT being a team player.

On May 13, 1994, the Bulls were fighting for their playoff lives in Game 3 against the Knicks, down 2-0 in the series. With 5.5 seconds left, Pippen waved for Kukoc to set a screen for him, which never materialized, and Pippen's contested heave that hit the top of the backboard ended up being a shot-clock violation. Ewing's hook tied the game at 102 with 1.8 seconds remaining. Then coach Phil Jackson designed the final play for Kukoc — with Pippen to inbound the ball. According to the New York Times, citing ESPN reporter Andrea Kramer, Pippen swore and said, "I'm tired of this," then sat on the bench and refused teammates imploring him to get up. Jackson had to call a second timeout. Pete Myers inbounded in Pippen's place and Kukoc hit the game-winner.[111]

Twenty-five years later, basketball fans and commentators still reference this event as an example of extreme selfishness and a lack of desire to fulfill one's role in a sporting event. Pippen decided he did not want to play the final 1.8 seconds of an important playoff game, because of what he deemed to be an inferior role on the final play. The article went on to say, "Scottie Pippen played 3,642 playoff minutes during his Hall of Fame career. But it's the 1.8 seconds of postseason action he skipped…that are never far from the public conscious."[112]

---

[111] Phil Thompson, "25 Years Ago, Scottie Pippen Defiantly Benched Himself in the Final 1.8 Seconds of a Playoff Game," Chicago Tribune, last modified May 13, 2019, accessed November 17, 2020, https://www.chicagotribune.com/sports/bulls/ct-spt-bulls-scottie-pippen-1994-playoffs-sits-20190513-story.html.

[112] Thompson, "25 Years Ago, Scottie Pippen."

So, some introductory comments are in order as we consider the distinct, yet valuable role that a wife plays in a marriage relationship. As mentioned before, although the roles in a marriage are different, the intrinsic value and worth of each person in the marriage relationship are completely the same before the Lord. They are both loved, valued, and accepted just the way they are IN Christ. Each person in a marriage relationship, if a believer in Jesus Christ, possesses all the resources possible IN Christ. They have grace resources and spiritual blessings in abundance (See Ephesians 1:3).

A lack of occupation with the Lord Jesus and His resources are what cause many of the struggles in marriage. Often, husbands and wives focus more on their perceived individual rights than they do on their own duties and roles in marriage. When husbands and wives become more focused on their spouses and their spouse's failure to fulfill their roles, they begin a slow and steady decline into an unhealthy view of marriage. God's Word teaches that men and women are equal. The matter of a wife's submission to her own husband is a related but still different than gender equality. Furthermore, while wives are subordinate to their own husbands in the position and outworking of the family, wives possess equal value to their husband in person and worth.[113] Dr. Steven Waterhouse, a pastor, Bible teacher, Christian author, and biblical counselor, states clearly in his book Husband and Wife: The Imitation of Christ, "The Bible *DOES NOT* teach that all women are subordinate to men, and submission in a marriage has nothing to do with gender equality!"[114] This is why, when we begin to look at Ephesians 5:22 and the biblical role and duty of a wife in marriage, context is critical. This text is specifically dealing with a wife within the confines of her marriage and NOT a woman within the confines of her society!

Now, many would agree and realize that Christ is the role model or example for husbands, but few realize that Christ is also the role model and example for wives! Consider the following verse in 1 Corinthians 11:3, which states, "But I want you to know that the head of every man is Christ, the head of woman is man, and the head of Christ is God," and the verse

---

[113] Steven W. Waterhouse, Husband and Wife: The Imitation of Christ, (Amarillo, Texas: Westcliff Press, 2012), 5.
[114] Waterhouse, Husband and Wife, 5.

in 1 Corinthians 15:28, which states, "Now when all things are made subject to Him, then the Son Himself will also be subject to Him who put all things under Him, that God may be all in all." Now, if the head of Jesus Christ is God the Father, and, if Jesus Christ is subject to God the Father, does that make Jesus Christ less than God? Of course not, but what it does describe are different roles and duties within the Godhead. While Jesus was on earth, He willingly emptied Himself of His divine prerogative to exercise His divine attributes, and He placed Himself under the leadership and direction of God the Father. Jesus literally "walked by faith" during His earthly ministry; hence, the reason why He said multiple times that He only speaks what His Father tells Him to speak, and He only does what His Father tells Him to do (See John 5:19, 30, 36; 7:16; 8:28, 38; 12:49-50; 14:10, 24). Waterhouse also writes of this unique relationship when he says the following, "The comparison of a wife to her husband is likened to God the Son in relationship to God the Father. God the Son is co-equal to His Father in Person and worth. Yet, in the work of the Trinity, the Son voluntarily chose to submit Himself to the Father. He remained equal in Person and worth but chose to submit in the position and work of the

Godhead. A Christian wife's role is to imitate the Lord Jesus Christ in His relationship to His Father."[115] D. Edmond Hiebert writes, "Submission to authority is often consistent with equality in importance, dignity, and honor – Jesus was subject both to his parents and to God the Father."[116] So, Jesus is just as big of an example for wives in the marriage relationship as He is for the husbands!

As we move into Ephesians 5:22-24, we must understand the context of the passage once again. Just as it was for the husbands, verse 18 is imperative for wives to understand in order to fulfill their roles. Ephesians 5:18 reads, "And do not be drunk with wine, in which is dissipation; but be filled with the Spirit." Simply put, in order to be biblical wives, wives must learn to walk by means of the Spirit and be filled by the Spirit. To attempt to execute the command to "submit to their own husbands" in their own strength, apart from the empowering work of the Spirt of God, would be an effort in futility for any wife, regardless of her

---

[115] Waterhouse, Husband and Wife, 19.
[116] D. Edmond Hiebert, 1 Peter, (Winona Lake, IN.: BMH Books, 1984), 195.

most ardent desire to do so. Consistency, stability, and faithfulness in this area can only be accomplished when a believing wife is filled by the Spirit with the life of Jesus Christ. As mentioned earlier, Jesus knows personally HOW to place Himself under someone's authority. So, verse 18, in relationship to a wife's role in marriage is absolutely essential to understand. Also, as we further consider the context, verse 21 speaks of the subjection/submission found among all Christians in the Church. Dr. Harold Hoehner, showing the connection between verses 21 and 22, writes the following in his commentary on Ephesians: "The last of the characteristics of believers filled by the Spirit is submission to one another, that is, in the midst of the body of believers. However, moving to the household code he restricts the command to wives alone."[117] So, now, when we get to verse 22, Paul specifically addresses how this subjection plays out in the marriage relationship.

---

[117] Harold W. Hoehner, Ephesians: An Exegetical Commentary, (Grand Rapids: Baker Academic, 2002), 733.

Ephesians 5:22 reads, "Wives, submit to your own husbands, as to the Lord." Now, contrary to popular belief, the word "submit" is NOT a six-letter curse word. The word itself means "to place in order; or to place under in an orderly fashion. It was a military term meaning "to line up in order."[118] Now, the reason that this is so difficult, and the reason it must be commanded with assumed divine resources is because this is in direct opposition to how women are naturally bent! Some may say, "Wait a minute! What are you saying about women or wives?" Well, based upon Genesis 3:16, we learn that a wife's natural desire is to rule OVER her husband, NOT to place herself UNDER her husband. Now, I am not saying this to be critical of women at all – I am simply trying to make wives aware of what they are up against. This is the natural bent of a wife's sin nature, and a wife needs to be aware of this. It is because of this natural wiring, due to the fall of mankind into sin, that verse 18 and being filled by the Spirit is also KEY for wives to function in a biblical and pleasing manner to the Lord.

---

[118] Zodhiates, The Complete Word Study Dictionary, 5293.

This is God's biblical mandate for a wife, and this was His original design for Eve. Women must understand that by signing up for marriage, they are signing up for this role. This is part of the job description if a marriage is going to function biblically, and it is not up for negotiation or revision! God has a certain order that He wants things done because He knows that marriage will work best when done in His way. This is ordered, according to divine thinking, and it involves the husband leading, AND the wife following her own husband. One thing that a wife must understand is that this approach (submission to her own husband) is what is best for a Spirit-led wife whether she realizes it or not! Similar to how the husband's obedience to the command in verse 25 benefits himself, so to this command to "submit" given to the wife is found in the **middle voice**, indicating that she does the action and the benefit of the action will come back on her! It is important to note that this command to wives is **NOT** in the **passive voice**, which could have communicated that she is forced, by an outside force, to submit against her will.[119][120] Nowhere in Scripture does the husband's role include forcing his wife to submit to him or force his wife into servitude. Homer Kent wrote, "Although he has told the wives to be in subjection, he does not tell the husbands to treat their wives as subjects."[121] Also, although he tells the husbands to love their wives, he

---

[119] There is a textual variant here regarding the command in 5:22 to "submit." In the Translation Notes of the NET Bible it reads, "The witnesses for the shorter reading (in which the verb "submit" is only implied) are minimal (𝔓⁴⁶ B Cl Hier^mss), but significant and early. The rest of the witnesses add one of two verb forms as required by the sense of the passage (picking up the verb from v. 21). Several of these witnesses have ὑποτασσέσθωσαν (*hupotassesthōsan*), the third person imperative (so ℵ A I P Ψ 0278 33 81 1175 1739 1881 *al* lat co), while other witnesses, especially the later Byzantine cursives, read ὑποτάσσεσθε (*hupotassesthe*), the second person imperative (D F G 𝔐 sy). The text virtually begs for one of these two verb forms, but the often cryptic style of Paul's letters argues for the shorter reading. The chronology of development seems to have been *no verb*—third person imperative—second person imperative. It is not insignificant that early lectionaries began a new day's reading with v. 22; these most likely caused copyists to add the verb at this juncture."

[120] Some (commentators) think this verb is passive…others suggest that this verb is middle…The passive could convey the idea that a person submits because he or she is forced to submit, for example, as one is submissive to a dictator; however, the middle definitely connotes that the subject volitionally exercises the action of submission, an act of a free agent. The middle seems in keeping with the context for three reason. First, there is no indication that the church's submission to Christ is forced. Second, the duty of the husband is phrased in the active imperative (v25)…Third, in the previous context (5:18-21), four out of the five participles dependent on the imperative "to be filled by the Spirit" are active and the fifth participle (submitting) is best seen as middle where the subject is responsible for the action. Therefore, the submissi0n here is better taken not as a passive but as a middle, with the wife acting as free agent before God. - Homer A. Kent, Jr., Ephesians: The Glory of the Church, (Chicago: Moody Publishers, 1971), 731-732.

[121] Ibid, 101.

does not tell the wives in turn to wait for their husbands to love them before they submit to him.

Wives need to understand that part of the motivation God is going to use in their husband's life to pursue them with **agape** love is their response of faith in placing themselves under him. When wives do this, this builds their husbands up — this puts a tremendous amount of courage and confidence in him, and it should sober him to know the responsibility and trust his wife is placing in him and cause him to recognize his need to trust the Lord. When he does this, he will be walking by means of the Spirit, and the Spirit of God will produce **agape** love in and through him, which will benefit the wife.

Unfortunately, what is so ironic, is the wife's sin nature will try to convince her to do everything just the opposite. Thus, wives, when walking according to the flesh, will attempt to control their husbands, manipulate their husbands, and do everything they need to do in order to get their way. Often, getting their way means "self-protection," alleviating fear and anxiety, and attempting to avoid difficult circumstances. Thus, their marriage relationship becomes more about controlling and avoiding adverse circumstances, and they never trust the Lord by placing themselves under the husband's leadership.

As we consider the topic of submission for the wives, it is probably helpful to look at what submission is **NOT** in order to provide extra clarification. First, "submission" is **NOT** an inferior position, status, or value. This reflects a role in marriage and describes the primary function for the wife in a marriage. Again, this role has nothing to do with your usefulness in the local church, the home, or in the community. 1 Peter 3:7 says that wives are co-heirs with their husbands, and thus their value and equality is on par with their husbands. Second, "submission" is **NOT** a wife who never disagrees with her husband or voices her opinions or concerns. A husband would be an absolute fool not to listen to his wife's concerns or her insights on situations in their lives. A submissive wife is not one who completely sits by and never contributes or engages on any day-to-day decisions regarding their lives together. She is, however, an active partner in discussing and providing perspective but does not think that the husband must choose her argument every time a decision is made in order for her to feel like she has been heard. Third, "submission" is **NOT** turning your brain "off" and going into drone-mode. "Yes, dear…yes, dear…yes, dear." For women to be biblical wives and walk by means of the Spirit, their minds must be actively engaged because they will be choosing to actively walk by faith in the truths of God's Word. So, the concept of submission, which says that "good" wives will be mindless, is completely off base and missing the point! Fourth, and it has been mentioned earlier, "submission" is **NOT** all women submitting to all men. This is one wife submitting to her own husband. Notice the phrase "**to your own husbands.**" This command is exclusive and is only found in the unique and special relationship ordained by God known as marriage. Fifth, "submission" is **NOT** a perch for the "I told you so's" of life. A wife's job is not to prevent her husband from making mistakes, but neither is it to point out and gloat in every mistake that he does make when he did not follow her counsel. Many women secretly root against their husbands when they make a decision that does not go right in line with their counsel. Thus, they seem to find great joy is telling him, "I told you so!" with the added implication, "Maybe you will listen to me next time!" They really mean the following: "Maybe you will submit to my leadership next time!" Sixth, "submission" is **NOT** just the right actions – meaning NOT verbally disagreeing and just doing what you are told, etc. It is a right attitude – meaning that wives are not rolling their eyes, not sighing heavily, and not just having a "whatever" attitude where they have pretty much given up and thrown in the towel.

So, for added clarity, what is "submission" biblically? First, "submission" for wives **IS** recognizing and trusting God's original design for marriage. For many women, this is scary! This is walking by faith in God's plan in what He says is best for the marriage. Wives have to be completely convinced that this is the ONLY way they can find true joy and fulfillment in their marriages. In fact, many times wives are going to need to trust God's Word above what they can see, and what they evaluate themselves. Wives must trust that God knows what He is doing, and He knows what is best for them. Second, "submission" for wives **IS** entrusting themselves to God by entrusting themselves to the leadership of fallen man (their husband). Dr. Steven Waterhouse makes a keen insight when he says, "A wife can appreciate her husband's intent without thinking the results will be superior."[122] Third, "submission" for wives **IS** diametrically opposed to what is "natural" for wives based on Genesis 3:16. Thus, the next phrase in verse 22 becomes a key insight into understanding HOW women can submit to their own husbands.

The text says that wives are to submit to their own husbands "as unto the Lord." Thus, submission to one's husband is really an act of worship and faith in the Lord. This phrase speaks to the mindset of the wife, where her focus is, and where her motivation springs from. This is a woman who is occupied with the Lord as she executes this command in her marriage. This is what a Spirit-filled wife looks like. As she submits to her husband, she is submitting to the Lord. This phrase, as unto the Lord, reminds us that wives do not submit to their husbands because their husbands are WORTHY to be submitted to. Often, their husbands are NOT worthy to be submitted to. This phrase, as unto the Lord, reminds us that wives do not submit to their husbands because their husbands are INTELLECTUALLY SUPERIOR to them. In fact, often, wives are

---

[122] Waterhouse, Husband and Wife, 16.

superior to their husbands intellectually. This phrase, as unto the Lord, reminds us that wives do not submit to their husbands because their husbands have more WISDOM than they do in life. Again, this is often the exact opposite in some marriages. This phrase, as unto the Lord, reminds us of WHY wives are to submit to their own husbands — because the Word of God commands it, and wives recognize that God is ultimately in charge and capable of leading their husbands and thus capable of leading and protecting them.

Because of this fact, wives DO NOT have to manipulate their husbands to maintain control and, thus, protect themselves. God is in this thing called marriage, and He wants to do these things for the wives. Can they trust Him to do it? Can they submit to their husbands as unto the Lord? Wives need to simply come alongside of their husbands and help and support them to become the men of God that God wants them to be. If your husband is walking by means of the Spirit, you will live in complete love and security. If wives learn to help their men blossom and flourish in their relationship with the Lord, they themselves will receive the direct benefit from it!

Now, Paul provides a reason for wives' submission to their own husbands in verse 23 — "For the husband is the head of the wife, as also Christ is head of the church; and He is the Savior of the body." The word translated "for" (**hoti**) further explains and expands the idea of WHY the wife should submit to her own husband as to the Lord. What is the reason given? "The husband is the head of the wife as also Christ is head of the church." This theological and God designed order is stated as a present tense and ongoing fact! Paul goes straight to a positional truth, which is unchanging even if we do not believe it. In other words, this is HOW God has set up the marriage relationship and structure, and it remains according to this set up. Now, the only reason someone would fight against this is because he or she thinks he or she knows better than God as to how marriage should work. There is a reason marriage is set up this way by God, and this is the reason that this set up, and this set up ALONE, can lead to a fulfilling, satisfying marriage.

This concept of **headship** is found other places as well (1 Corinthians 11:3) where it communicates that the "head" of the woman is man, the "head" of the man is Christ, and the "head" of Christ is God.

Man's headship over woman no more implies that woman is inferior to man, as does the Father's headship over Christ imply that Christ is inferior to the Father. There is a hierarchical set up within the Godhead where Christ submits to the Father, and, thus, superiority or inferiority is **NOT** even the issue here! God's order and being orderly **IS** the issue! Humility recognizes that God knows how to design things, order things, and He does it all well! So, when we consider headship, it implies a couple of things: leadership, accountability, and responsibility. This is everything Adam was **NOT** in the garden as he watched the serpent lie and deceive Eve, but, in contrast, this is everything Christ **IS** for the Church! Again, husbands can function biblically if and only if they are filled by the Spirit with the life of Jesus Christ. Many husbands love the idea of being a leader because in their mind it gives them the right to tell their wives what to do, but husbands often forget the other qualities of headship – accountability and responsibility. This means when a husband makes a mistake in leading, he takes personal responsibility for it. He alone takes accountability and does not blame his wife for her faults. Husbands who blame their spouses for everything are NOT leaders, and they are NOT functioning well in their roles as heads of the family.

Going back to verse 23, we also see that Christ alone is the "Savior of the body." Notice here Paul does not make a "just as" comparison to the husband. He simply says Christ is the "Savior of the body" and NOT that the husband is the "Savior of his wife." This is an interesting observation! First, before exploring this observation, a "Savior" by definition is a deliverer, a preserver, and one who saves from danger or destruction and brings into a state of prosperity and happiness. Jesus alone can do this! This is WHY Paul does NOT make the "just as" comparison with this phrase, and it factors into WHY every believing wife can submit to her own husband as to the Lord. Ultimately, Jesus and Jesus ALONE is her Savior! This means each wife's husband is NOT her Savior, he is NOT her deliverer, NOR is he capable or able to meet all her needs. Hence, the command to place oneself under her husband is for the wife only possible as she sees that she is ultimately trusting the Lord by willingly obeying this command.

Now, Paul does use a "just as" comparison in verse 24, which says, "Therefore, just as the church is subject to Christ, so let the wives be to their own husbands in everything." When considering the word, "therefore," here it is important to note that it is NOT the typical Greek word translated "therefore." This word is the Greek word **alla**, which is typically translated "but" to serve as a marked opposition to what was stated before.[123] However, when the word is used to further communicate or build upon what was said before, it can mean **but still more**. This provides an emphatic conclusion to what was communicated in verses 22-23. So, when Paul says, "just as the church is subject to Christ," he is communicating that the Church **IS** subject to Christ whether or not the Church realizes it or not. The Church is subject to Christ whether or not she always acts in accordance with that truth. This is God's order, design, and desire for both the Church and for wives. Now, just as…this is to be the same with wives and their own husbands because this is God's ordained way.

---

[123] Zodhiates, The Complete Word Study Dictionary, 235.

Now, Paul adds further clarification and teaching when he uses the phrase "in everything." Many wives may be thinking, "**REALLY?** In **EVERYTHING?**" In short, the answer is "Yes!" The ultimate goal of the wife's submission is to be in every facet of her family life, in relationship to her husband, and in his leading. If this is the mindset of the woman, then she is NOT easily distracted or disturbed by what she might view as an UNWISE or FOOLISH decision by her husband. She is, by faith, trusting the Lord through her husband, knowing that he will NOT make perfect decisions all the time. Many women race to the potential exceptions of when they should NOT submit to their husbands, but you will notice that Paul NEVER races to the exception clauses in any other area of authority structures in normal human life. With the authority structure of human government in Romans 13:1-7, Paul mentions no exception clause. With parents and their authority over their children in Ephesians 6:1, Paul mentions no exception clause. With employers and employees in Ephesians 6:5, Paul mentions no exception clause. This is important to observe because the general mindset of believers is to simply trust the Lord to work in each of these situations and NOT to always be on the lookout for when someone else violates their roles or duties. If a wife is constantly looking for an exception to her having to "submit to her husband," she will live a distracted life and will find it difficult to consistently rely on the Lord to execute this command.

Although, it is not clearly spelled out in this passage but alluded to, there is at least one potential exception for the wife in submitting to her husband. If the husband is asking the wife to do something clearly in violation with God's Word, her higher responsibility will always be to God. This is why verse 22 adds the phrase "as to the Lord." We know from other scriptural examples that wives will be held accountable for their own actions before the Lord even when supposedly "submitting" to their husbands. Consider the account found in Acts 5:1-9, and the tragic story of a believing couple, Ananias and Sapphira. Sapphira apparently "submitted" to the leadership of her husband who had devised a deceitful story to the apostles in Jerusalem. When questioned, Sapphira went along with the lie and deceit of her husband, and she faced the same consequences as he did – death.

As we jump down to Ephesians 5:33, we pick up another instructive comment for the wives when it says, "Nevertheless let each one of you in particular so love his own wife as himself, and let the wife see that she respects her husband." The word "respect" means to put in fear, terrify, or frighten. It also means respect, awe, and reverence.[124] In terms of context, it seems better to understand this word in terms of respect, reverence and honor rather than to be frightened. So, this attitude and approach to their own husbands, is something that believing wives should do in a **continual** and **ongoing** manner. This is a mindset and lifestyle for them, and something that, if done, the text tells us they will receive the benefit of that action because it is given in the **middle voice**. So, for the wives, rather than fearing things in life and trying to take control, they can transfer that "respect" to their own husbands, entrusting themselves to their care. The idea communicated is that the wife is not in control, and she is to look to her husband to lead. Again, this speaks more to an INTERNAL response than merely just a proper and acceptable EXTERNAL response! This is exactly what a wife will look like **IF** she is filled by the Spirit (verse 18)

---

[124] Zodhiates, The Complete Word Study Dictionary, 5399.

because this is what the life of Jesus Christ, manifested through the wife's mortal body, will look like.

An additional passage in Colossians 3:18 provides further instruction for the wives when it says, "Wives, submit to your own husbands, as is fitting in the Lord." At first glance, it seems as if this verse is saying the exact same thing as Ephesians 5:22. In fact the same word "submit" is used, and it is used in the same exact Greek form as it was in Ephesians 5:22 (present, middle, imperative). But, the phrase, "as is fitting in the Lord," gives us additional subtle insight. The word translated "fitting" means what belongs, or what is proper, or what is fitting, or what is right. This instruction fits with the phrase, "as to the Lord," in Ephesians 5:22, but its subtle distinction is that this approach by a wife to her husband is the right FIT for her marriage. In other words, this type of response to her husband (submission) is the right part, the right fit, to get the job done. It is exactly what is needed from the wife in order for her to do her part in building a fulfilling, thriving marriage. This is the wife's "buy-in" that what God says is good, right, and proper for a marriage relationship is indeed the best way! This is the RIGHT WAY to go about it, regardless of what worldly wisdom teaches or encourages.

As with the role of husbands, what a high calling and privilege it is to be a wife! God is calling wives to a higher plane that can only be reached by utilizing the resources God provides. May wives be convinced of two things: (1) God wants to meet their needs and protect them, so they can entrust themselves to the care of a fallen and imperfect husband. They do not have to protect themselves, and (2) The only way to consistently place themselves under their husband's leadership is to be motivated by the fact that, as they do so, they are doing what they do as unto the Lord. As husbands were reminded in their section, 2 Corinthians 4:10-11 aptly deals with the difficulties of life, including marriage, and describes the benefit of walking by faith even when things are difficult. It reads, "Always carrying about in the body the dying of the Lord Jesus, **that the life of Jesus also may be manifested in our body.** For we who live are always delivered to death for Jesus' sake, **that the life of Jesus also may be manifested in our mortal flesh.**"

CHAPTER 10
HOW TO BE A BIBLICAL WIFE PART 2

Additional Scriptures contribute to our understanding of what a biblical wife looks like. It cannot be emphasized enough that it is NOT in trying to become a better wife that a woman becomes a biblical wife; it is when that woman, cognizant of her own lack of resources to submit or place herself under her husband in a biblical way, begins to trust in the Lord and be filled by His Spirit that she will begin to function biblically as a wife. This can happen in the first year of marriage, even on the first day! It can also happen when a believing wife, who has walked carnally for years, realizes her need for God's grace resources and begins, in that moment, to rely upon the Spirit of God to produce the life of Christ in and through her.

1 Peter 3:1-6 is another passage that emphasizes and further develops the concept of the wife's responsibility for biblical submission within her marriage. Dr. Constable, in his notes on 1 Peter, records a statement from a Family Life Conference that summarizes the further explanation of biblical submission in this passage. It reads:

> Submission involves at least four things. First, it begins with an attitude of entrusting oneself to God (cf. 2:23–25). The focus of our life must be on Jesus Christ. Second, submission requires respectful behavior (3:1–2). Nagging is not respectful behavior. Third, submission involves the development of a godly character (3:3–5). Fourth, submission includes doing what is right (3:6). It does not include violating other Scriptural principles. Submission is imperative for oneness in marriage.[125]

Submission in a marriage will be further expanded upon in these six verses in 1 Peter. 1 Peter 3:1-2 reads, "Wives, likewise, *be* submissive to your own husbands, that even if some do not obey the word, they, without a word, may be won by the conduct of their wives, when they observe your chaste conduct *accompanied* by fear." Now, to set the stage for the passage, we must first consider the context. Constable provides this helpful insight: "In that society women were expected to follow the religion of their husbands; they

---

[125] Tom Constable, "Notes on 1 Peter," *Plano Bible Chapel*, last modified 2020, accessed November 17, 2020, https://www.planobiblechapel.org/tcon/notes/html/nt/1peter/1peter.htm.

might have their own cult on the side, but the family religion was that of the husband. Peter clearly focuses his address on women whose husbands are not Christians (not that he would give different advice to women whose husbands were Christians), and he addresses them as independent moral agents whose decision to trust Christ he supports and whose goal to win their husbands he encourages. This is quite a revolutionary attitude for that culture."[126]

This background is helpful as we begin to dig into this passage. When dealing with the role of husbands a couple of chapters ago, we made note of the word "likewise" and its impact on the instruction to husbands in verse 7. The same note must be made here with the use of the word "likewise" in verse 1 because the use of the word begs the question – "What is Peter referring back to?" In this case, we trace it back to chapter two, which details the example of Jesus Christ in how He endured suffering. Notice what Peter records in 1 Peter 2:21-25 (**specifically verse 23**): "For to this you were called, because Christ also suffered for us, leaving us an

---

[126]Constable, "Notes on 1 Peter."

example, that you should follow His steps: *'Who committed no sin, nor was deceit found in His mouth';* **who, when He was reviled, did not revile in return; when He suffered, He did not threaten, but committed Himself to Him who judges righteously**; who Himself bore our sins in His own body on the tree, that we, having died to sins, might live for righteousness — by whose stripes you were healed. For you were like sheep going astray but have now returned to the Shepherd and Overseer of your souls." What can be gathered about Christ's example is that He did not seek to defend Himself, but rather He "entrusted Himself" to Him (i.e, the Father) who judges righteously. What is interesting is the wording used here: "committed Himself" or "entrusted Himself," as it relates to judgment. When people "reviled" Jesus or "persecuted" Jesus, they were passing a judgment of some sort on Him. They were in essence saying to Jesus, "You deserve the punishment you are receiving." What is really fascinating about this is that Jesus NEVER did anything wrong, so if there were ONE person in the history of the world who did **NOT** ever deserve to be judged as a lawbreaker, it was Jesus Christ. Thus, he was being judged incorrectly, and His punishment was a serious miscarriage of true justice. It is also interesting to note that the word "commit" or "entrust" is used all throughout the trial of Jesus to describe how He was "given over" to someone's jurisdiction for trial. As they transferred Jesus to and from his multiple trials, this word is used. Additionally, this SAME word is often translated "betray" or "betrayal," as in the case of Judas. Hence, what does the semantic range of meaning for this Greek word tell us? Simply, it tells us that Jesus Christ betrayed Himself to God by removing all forms and efforts to self-protect and self-defend. Now, women, in the same way or "likewise," entrust yourselves to a perfect God while submitting to an imperfect man.

Let's be honest – for wives to submit to their husbands, while entrusting themselves to God is a very scary proposition. In fact, when you consider the outcome of Jesus entrusting Himself to God in the face of persecution, He still suffered tremendously. The encouragement to wives here is beyond just the moment and looks ahead to things of eternal value when all things will be measured and evaluated accurately. With this in mind, wives need to have a mentally settled attitude that they will **NOT** go into self-protection mode in their marriage. When I say self-protection, I am speaking of protecting one's feelings, one's pride, defending oneself, railing and reviling their husband, and ultimately making the decision that they must protect themselves, or NO ONE else will. Peter encourages wives to entrust themselves to the Lord and to allow God to protect them and take care of their husband.

Now that we have the "likewise" covered, what are the wives instructed to do with this mindset that Jesus had? Peter tells them to "be submissive," which is the same word Paul uses in Ephesians 5:22 and Colossians 3:18. Again, the word simply means to place in order OR to place under in an orderly fashion. Now, what is slightly different with its use here is that Peter uses this word in the **passive voice**. This implies that the wives are not doing this action, but rather this action is happening **TO** them by an outside source. What is interesting about this is that as we take the concept of "entrusting oneself to God," and combine the passive use of wives being submissive to their own husbands, it indicates that, as the wives volitionally choose to entrust themselves to the Lord, this act of faith will put them in submission to their husbands. If there were ever a "how to submit" section in Scripture, this is it! By entrusting themselves to the Lord, wives, actively trusting the Lord, will be in submission to their own husbands.

Sounds good, but it begs the question – What if the wife's husband is not saved? Does she still need to submit to this type of husband? We could take these questions a step further in Christian marriages as well: What if the wife's husband IS saved, but he is carnal most of the time and has no interest in walking with the Lord or growing spiritually? What if he would rather stay home and watch college football? Work on the car? Etc. Peter addresses these thoughts here in the next phrase, "even if some do not obey the word." In context, Peter is most likely referencing "unbelieving" husbands, but, as mentioned above, the same could apply to husbands who are saved, yet living carnally (like an unbeliever). The word translated "do not obey" (**apeitheo**) means not allowing oneself to be persuaded or to believe.[127] Individuals either have not believed the gospel (they are unsaved), or they have believed the gospel (they are saved) but they are not trusting the Lord in their daily lives (they are carnal Christians).

---

[127] Zodhiates, The Complete Word Study Dictionary, 544.

Now, notice the response Peter encourages here regardless of either one of these scenarios – entrust yourselves to God, being submissive. Would this response by the wives harm them in the long run, or would it cause the wives to be perpetual doormats, or could something positive actually be the result?

Peter says that something very positive could result in the proper response of the wife – her husband could be won! The phrase "they may be won" means literally "to gain or acquire as gain."[128] This most likely refers to the husband being led to the Lord for salvation or maybe becoming convinced to trust the Lord in his daily life. Constable makes a good point when he says, "Peter did not promise that unbelieving husbands would inevitably become Christians as a result of the behavior he prescribed. That decision lies with the husband. Nevertheless, the wife can have confidence that she has been faithful to God if she relates to her husband submissively."[129]

---

[128] Zodhiates, The Complete Word Study Dictionary, 2770.
[129] Constable, "Notes on 1 Peter."

However, **HOW** can a wife do this practically? By nagging? By manipulating him to go to church? By bribing him to attend a Bible study? By talking about Bible verses and forcing family devotions on him? By writing verses all over his computer, briefcase, or sock drawer? By changing his radio stations in his car to Christian radio? Some of these may be okay if the husband is responsive to this, but this is not the emphasis from Peter. His emphasis is rather, **WITHOUT** a word (non-verbal), by the wife's conduct. The biblical emphasis is on the wife relating to the husband submissively, showing him honor and respecting him and his position in the home. This is a lifestyle, NOT a special event or a little extra **SUGAR** from time to time but an ongoing settled disposition. A great example of this type of godly submission with positive results is found in the historical account of Augustine's mother:

> Monica was married to a pagan official named Patritius, who had a short temper and lived an immoral life. At first, her mother-in-law did not like her, but Monica won her over by her gentle disposition. Unlike many women of that time, St. Monica was never beaten by her husband. She said that Patritius never raised his hand against

her because she always held her tongue, setting a guard over her mouth in his presence. It was a source of great pain that Patritius would not permit their children to be baptized. She worried about Augustine, who lived with a young woman in Carthage who bore him an illegitimate son. Her constant prayers and tears for her son had the effect of converting her husband to Christ before his death.[130]

Now, for many women, this may seem backwards. This way may seem to be the only way to ensure failure and to ensure a lack of change in one's husband. Yet, many times in the word of God, God's way appears backwards. Sometimes the way up is down. Sometimes the way right is left. Sometimes, God appears to flip things right on their head, where it does not make any sense to our common logic. Thus, if the wife will simply trust the Lord and His word and rely upon Him, He can do things that she never thought were possible.

---

[130] Orthodox Church in America, "St. Monica, Mother of Augustine of Hippo," Antiochian Orthodox Christian Archdiocese of North America, last modified 2020, accessed November 18, 2020, http://ww1.antiochian.org/node/18343.

What is interesting is that Peter says that this type of approach – being submissive and exhibiting consistent conduct without a lot of chatter – is observable by a woman's husband. In verse two, Peter describes the wife's conduct in two ways and says that this conduct is "observable," meaning the husband looks upon the conduct of the wife with the result of contemplating it.[131] In other words, the husband takes note of this settled disposition. The first of two things the husband takes note of specifically concerning his wife is her "chaste conduct," meaning freedom from defilements or impurities.[132] D. Edmond Hiebert defines this word as "innocence refined by testing."[133] In other words, there is no manipulation, and no ulterior motives emanating from the wife. What you see is what you get with her. She is free from all this "double agent" behavior in a pure manner of living — she relates well and transparently with her husband – she does not deceive him or try to trick him into certain things. She is not flirtatious and does not look to get her emotional needs met somewhere

---

[131] Zodhiates, The Complete Word Study Dictionary, 2029.
[132] Zodhiates, The Complete Word Study Dictionary, 53.
[133] D. Edmond Hiebert, 1 Peter, (Winona Lake, IN: BMH Books, 1984), 198.

else and by someone else, while all the while pretending to be transparent and wholly devoted to her husband. When a wife DOES NOT behave in this way, she communicates, even without words, that the husband will never make right decisions on his own; thus, she needs to manipulate and control the decisions he is making, so he does not make any mistakes leading the family. Husbands may not pick up all the subtleties in their marriage, but they can quickly detect a lack of purity in how their wife relates to them. This lack of "chaste conduct" is then interpreted by most husbands as a threat to their authority, value, and capability as the leader of the home. Most men do not respond well to this type of challenge.

The second of two things husbands take note of specifically concerning their wives is their "fear," meaning fear, terror, reverence, respect, honor.[134] This word is often used in Scripture to communicate these last few ideas of respect and honor. This is how the verb form of this word was used in Ephesians 5:33, regarding wives' response to their husbands. In this case, it is important to note that husbands respond well

---

[134] Zodhiates, The Complete Word Study Dictionary, 5401.

to being looked to — husbands respond well to being their wife's hero — husbands respond well to their wife's loving respect of them. In fact, many husbands will step up and take the responsibility if honor and respect is given to them by their wives. It is ironic that this positive, respectful response can actually motivate a man to want to be better. However, when wives disrespect their husbands, think they can do it better than they can, or they criticize their husbands for making a mistake, their conduct exposes their lack of submission. Thus, wives, to show respect and honor for the position your husband has in the family, you are recognizing God's plan for the family. This is HOW wives do the "LIKEWISE" thing even though it may be uncomfortable! This alone has the ability to work wonders in a husband and wife's relationship because this submission will encourage, build up, and strengthen the husband. And, as these two verses indicate, the husband may be profoundly impacted in a positive way, and it has the potential to prompt the husband to take his God-given role seriously and begin to look for ways to fulfill it according to God's design.

Now, verses three and four take a little bit of a turn in focus as Peter writes, "Do not let your adornment be merely outward – arranging the hair, wearing gold, or putting on fine apparel – rather let it be the hidden person of the heart, with the incorruptible beauty of a gentle and quiet spirit, which is very precious in the sight of God." Here Peter really hones in on a typical response of some women, which is to control, manipulate, or influence their husband through their outward appearance. In our culture, I feel sorry for women in general and for wives specifically. Our culture pushes and promotes external beauty relentlessly, and women of all shapes and sizes are continually fighting against this imaginary "beauty stick" of airbrushing and photoshopped "beauty." It is very disheartening to see the way Satan has swayed this world system in such an overwhelmingly influential way. However, this is NOT unique to our modern culture, as Peter points out in his Roman culture. When women begin to realize that their husband is not responding to them, many immediately turn to external appearance as a means to regain control and/or influence over their husbands. Peter is going to tell the Christian wife – do not buy into this type of carnal thinking because Christian wives have something much more valuable to offer their husbands! They can offer the life of Jesus Christ in and through their mortal flesh, and this **IS** exactly what husbands need from their wives.

When Peter says, "Do not let your adornment be *merely* outward," he is negating the present tense command. This means that Peter could be commanding the wives to "stop an action already in progress" or to "not even start an action." This Greek form emphasizes urgency and immediacy! There is no time to waste in Peter's thinking for the wives to begin to apply this truth. The word translated "adornment" actually translsates the Greek word **kosmos.** This word means "world, to order, to set in order, to adorn, or to garnish."[135] It was used of decorating sepulchers, setting a household in order, referencing someone or something's regular disposition, and describing an arrangement. Literally, one could say to the wives, "Do not let your normal 'world' be merely outwardly focused." External appearance can drive everything a woman does in her life if external appearance is her **WORLD**! Notice the specific things that Peter mentions: It is arranging the hair, wearing gold, and putting on fine apparel. We could add in our day: Working out for a "beach body," getting the best "make up," going under the knife for plastic surgery, getting Botox injections, or any other

---

[135] Zodhiates, The Complete Word Study Dictionary, 2889.

outwardly focused item that our culture promotes! Our culture takes more pictures with the camera facing us (selfies) than we do facing out, and this is just an indicator of the externally-focused mindset and culture that is easy to get sucked into.

Now, before we go too far off the reservation and go to another unbiblical extreme, it might be wise to discuss what this is NOT saying: (1) Wives, let yourselves go on the outside, OR (2) Wives, you cannot wear nice clothes or jewelry OR (3) Wives, do not practice normal standards of hygiene. What is ironic about this whole passage is that a host of legalistic-minded Christians have taken this passage and have ran with it! They will teach it is sinful to wear nice clothes, make-up, jewelry, or any type of fancy outward apparel. This is **<u>NOT</u>** what this passage is saying at all! Legalism always focuses on controlling externals, and what is ironic is that legalists are doing the exact thing that Peter says NOT to do here. They are focused on externals as a means of accomplishing something! Chuck Swindoll perfectly summarizes a balanced view when he says, "Peter merely wants to put those things in the background and bring the woman's character into

How to be a Biblical Wife Part 2   249

the foreground. Perspective is the key."[136] Peter's instruction implies that if a wife's world is outward appearance, she will have a harder time being focused on what **TRULY** matters (submission to her husband and fulfilling God's biblical design for marriage). Outward adornment can become a major distraction and can negatively influence the quality of her marriage. Even though she is putting forth a lot of effort, it is effort put in the wrong direction.

What is Peter saying then? He **IS** saying: (1) Do not let outward appearance dominate your focus in life, (2) Do not look for approval or acceptance from your husband based upon your external appearance, and (3) You, as a wife, can give your husband something **SO MUCH BETTER** than a nice outward appearance! In fact, outward beauty and adorning is implied in verse 4 to be "corruptible," meaning "destruction, spoil, or to subvert."[137] Warren Wiersbe creatively writes, "Beauty must

---

[136] Charles R. Swindoll, Hope in Hurtful Times: A Study of 1 Peter, (Anaheim, CA.: Insight for Living, 1990), 56.
[137] Zodhiates, The Complete Word Study Dictionary, 862.

come from the heart and NOT the store."[138] Everyone knows that external beauty is temporary, and that external beauty in and of itself cannot sustain a marriage. If it could, then everyone in Hollywood would stay married!

This is why Peter goes on to tell women what they should be adorning themselves with in verse 4, "Rather *let it be* the hidden person of the heart, with the incorruptible *beauty* of a gentle and quiet spirit, which is very precious in the sight of God." The word "adorn" is implied here from verse 3, and the emphasis is "Let the hidden person of the heart with a gentle and quiet spirit be your **world**..." So, in contrast to having an external focus, Peter exhorts wives to have an internal focus. Literally, Peter is exhorting them to pay attention to and to let their spiritual life and health dominate their focus. Many times in marriage, it is easy for a wife to allow her husband to dominate her focus – what he IS doing, and what he IS NOT doing – and yet here Peter says to pay attention to your spiritual health and well-being. More specifically, let your occupation with Jesus

---

[138] Warren W. Wiersbe, Be Hopeful: How to Make the Best of Times Out of Your Worst of Times, (Colorado Springs: Chariot Victor Publishing,1982), 72.

Christ be your focus, instead of corruptible things like external beauty.[139] Wives need to make sure that this, and this ALONE, is their occupation! Wives can do other things (even work out, fix their hair, wear nice clothes, etc.), but they are to never let these things become their **WORLD**!

To further expand on this phrase "the hidden person of the heart," this is what Paul refers to elsewhere as the "inner man" (Ephesians 3:16) or "inward man" (Romans 7:22; 2 Corinthians 4:16). This is referencing our new nature, which is empowered to shine forth by the indwelling Spirit of God. We learn a few things about our "inner man" or new nature from the Scriptures: First, our inner man needs to be strengthened. Paul's prayer in Ephesians 3:14-16 reveals this, " For this reason I bow my knees to the Father of our Lord Jesus Christ, from whom the whole family in heaven and earth is named, that He would grant you, according to the riches of His glory, to be strengthened with might through His Spirit in the inner man." This strengthening comes through things outside of the believer's control

---

[139] Having to exhibit godly behavior when their husbands are not, however, produces another tendency – substituting secret manipulation for a quiet spirit…pouting, sulking, scheming, bargaining, nagging, preaching, coercing, humiliating. – Swindoll, Hope in Hurtful Times, 55-56.

(circumstances, trials, difficult spouses) and requires the believer's participation via faith in the Lord and His resources. Notice, the strengthening here comes from the Spirit of God, and thus can only be benefited from as the believer relies upon Him. Second, our inner man loves God's law but cannot execute the righteous standard of the Law. Paul writes of his experience in this area in Romans 7:22-23, "For I delight in the law of God according to the inward man. But I see another law in my members, warring against the law of my mind, and bringing me into captivity to the law of sin which is in my members." This should remind every believer that just having the right desires is not enough to execute those desires. The Spirit of God must enable believers to live righteously. Third, our inner man is being renewed by God every day. Paul affirms this in 2 Corinthians 4:16, "Therefore we do not lose heart. Even though our outward man is perishing, yet the inward *man* is being renewed day by day." This is encouraging! God is at work here, and He is relentlessly and proactively strengthening the inner man in each and every believer, including wives. So, if God is putting this much effort and attention on a wife's "hidden person of the heart," shouldn't she?

Now, one noticeable result will manifest itself when a wife adorns or "makes her world" the hidden person of the heart according to Peter. Her inner beauty will be "incorruptible," meaning not capable of corruption.[140] This truth is given in direct contrast to outward beauty, which does go away as you get older. Additionally, it is this type of beauty, which is described as "very precious" to God. The Greek word translated "very precious" means very expensive, very costly, and the idea communicated is that it has extreme value![141] God views beauty a completely different way than the world does, and His view is the only one that matters. When God sees a wife, He is not caught up with her externals, but rather what is going on "under the hood," and what is going on internally and spiritually. Peter goes on to describe this beauty with two adjectives: gentle and quiet. This is not describing a wife who is silent, never speaks, never voices her opinion, or just sits in a corner keeping to herself. Hiebert defines these two words the following way, "Gentle means she will not be pushy or

---

[140] Zodhiates, The Complete Word Study Dictionary, 862.
[141] Zodhiates, The Complete Word Study Dictionary, 4185.

selfishly assertive, rather she will be considerate and unassuming in her relations with her husband. Quiet means a spirit, which calmly bears the disturbances created by others and which itself does not create disturbances."[142] These two words are the opposite of being pushy, it is the opposite of being selfishly assertive, or getting one's own way at any cost. These words simply describe a wife who is filled by the Spirit and manifests and exemplifies the character of the life of Jesus Christ.

Now, Peter is going to provide a Scriptural example from the Old Testament and general unnamed examples from the past. Verses 5-6 read, "For in this manner, in former times, the holy women who trusted in God also adorned themselves, being submissive to their own husbands, as Sarah obeyed Abraham, calling him lord, whose daughters you are if you do good and are not afraid with any terror." By using the phrase "for in this manner," Peter is telling wives how to grow the hidden person of the heart and how to have a gentle and quiet spirit. In fact, he will tie adornment together with two practical concepts.

---

[142] Hiebert, 1 Peter, 201.

Holy women of the past did two things to **ADORN** the hidden person of the heart, their inner self. First, they **trusted/hoped** in God. This reminds Peter's audience that their "world" should first be vertical! As wives put their confident expectation in God and entrust themselves to Him, they will be able to follow their imperfect husbands. God will honor wives who do so and provide grace to handle any situation, stage of life, etc. that their husbands lead them into. Second, women in the past lived in **submission** to their own husbands. Once their "world" is vertical, they are much better oriented, mentally, to execute their horizontal responsibilities. What is implied is that when wives are vertically focused (they make their fellowship with the Lord their world), the horizontal responsibilities to their husbands will be a natural outflow. So, we see that adornment of the hidden person of the heart coincides with trusting in the Lord and being submissive to one's own husband. They all go together for a Christian wife, and thus a lack of submission on the part of a wife indicates that she is **NOT** trusting in the Lord!

Thus, in summary for the wives: (1) Submit to your own husbands as unto the Lord, and (2) Pursue the God-approved type of beauty and make your spiritual life and growth your "world." Again, as one final reminder and exhortation to the wives – wives cannot do this effectively or consistently if they are not walking by means of the Spirit. Wives, you, too, need to be spiritual to obey – you need to be spiritual to execute your divine roles and divinely-given duties!

CHAPTER 11

CLOSING THOUGHTS AND ENCOURAGEMENTS

To those who are ALREADY married: I am praying for you and your marriage as I write this. Marriage is designed by God to be the most fulfilling human to human relationship that exists in all of His creation. Unfortunately, for many, what was designed by God to be a fulfilling dream, has become a real, living nightmare! In light of the real problems that relational difficulties can cause in marriage, the upside is well worth pursuing – a relationship of love and respect, which supports one another physically, mentally, emotionally, and spiritually. Marriage provides a best friend, who is also your one and only lover, and the guaranteed one person on earth who wants your "best." What a blessing marriage can be when executed by means of God's Spirit!

Because marriage is one of the key building blocks of God's created order, it is imperative for each one of us, equipped by the Holy Spirit, to live moment-by-moment, relying upon God's resources alone in our marriages. Imagine the following:

(1) Marriages with both husband and wife consistently walking by means of the Spirit, producing disciples and future disciple-makers through their children.

(2) Marriages with both husband and wife consistently walking by means of the Spirit, impacting and blessing local churches through their families.

(3) Marriages with both husband and wife consistently walking by means of the Spirit, impacting local communities by their faithful witness and example of love and light.

Would this NOT be incredible? Would this NOT be rare? May your marriage become the "rarest" marriage in your entire extended family – until another marriage in your family becomes as "rare" as yours. May your marriage become the "rarest" marriage in your church family – until another marriage in your church family becomes as "rare" as yours. May your marriage become the "rarest" marriage in your community – until another marriage in your community becomes as "rare" as yours. May this continue to spread one marriage at a time, as every spouse in a marriage relationship looks to the Lord to fulfill their God-ordained roles in marriage. May your marriage thrive, not just survive! There is Hope, and His name is Jesus! Will you personally, regardless of how your spouse responds to you or to the Lord, begin to respond solely to the Lord and trust Him with the results? May He meet all your needs as you depend on Him!

To those who are NOT YET married: I will have to admit that one of the things I have often wanted to say in some of my marriage counselings is: "You guys should **NEVER** have gotten married!" Unfortunately, for many marriages in trouble, had the couple observed, NOT "blown through" the warning signs, during the dating period, they could have been spared the difficulties they now face. Clearly, in the present, God would have them work through their issues by His grace and resources, but had they, as single believers, trusted the Lord with their future, they may not have ended up in a depressing, trouble marriage relationship. A couple of quick hitting encouragements and exhortations:

> (1) Do not be in a hurry! Trust me, God knows all about your biological clock, knows all your childhood dreams, and knows how old you are getting (by the way, 25 is NOT old – neither is

30)! It is better to wait on God's timing for this decision – probably more so than any other decision you will make in your entire life!

(2) Be convinced, as you wait, that God wants your best! He wants to bless you with a fulfilling marriage – one that brings Him the utmost glory!

(3) Regardless of whether you are married or not, your primary focus and goal in life is a person – Jesus Christ, Himself. Occupy yourself with Him and thus become the type of "potential" Spirit-filled man or woman that other "potential" Spirit-filled men or women will be looking for themselves! As you walk in relational intimacy with Jesus Christ, you will naturally bump into and interact with others who are doing the same – that is a GREAT swimming pool to wade in when you are looking for a spouse.

May God give you, my presently single reader, a blessed experience of you trusting Him and then Him "showing up" and "showing out" for you in the provision of a spouse – one who encourages you towards greater intimacy with Him! May you be encouraged to wait on God's "good and perfect gift" in a spouse! Finally, may God richly meet all your needs in the time period while you wait!

For all: I close with the words of the apostle Paul in 2 Corinthians 5:14-15, which apply to every aspect of our lives: "For the love of Christ compels us, because we judge thus: that if One died for all, then all died; and He died for all, that those who live should live no longer **for themselves, but for Him** who died for them and rose again."

SCRIPTURE INDEX

Genesis 1:28, **25**
Genesis 2:18-20, **14**
Genesis 2:24, **190**
Genesis 2:25, **33**
Genesis 3:16, **214**, **221**
Genesis 3:1-7, **30**
Genesis 3:7-19, **32**
Genesis 3:7-8, **33**
Genesis 4:7, **39**
Exodus 19:7-8, **173**
Deuteronomy 7:2-4, **106**
2 Chronicles 20:1-12, **155**
Proverbs 1:10-19, **95**
Proverbs 1:5, **94**
Proverbs 1:7, **89**
Proverbs 1:8-9, **93**
Proverbs 11:22, **134**
Proverbs 12:1, **98**, **156**
Proverbs 12:11, **136**
Proverbs 12:15, **94**, **152**
Proverbs 12:4, **132**
Proverbs 15:1, **62**, **63**
Proverbs 15:25, 33; 16:18-19; 18:12; 29:23, **155**
Proverbs 15:4, **146**, **148**
Proverbs 17:17, **96**
Proverbs 18:13, **51**
Proverbs 19:1, **149**, **150**
Proverbs 19:13, **126**
Proverbs 20:19, **98**
Proverbs 21:19, **125**
Proverbs 21:25, **140**

Proverbs 21:9, **125**
Proverbs 25:19, **141**
Proverbs 25:24, **125**
Proverbs 26:20, **98**
Proverbs 27:15-16, **127**
Proverbs 28:13, **150**
Proverbs 3:5-6, **68**, **78**
Proverbs 31:30, **89**, **129**, **130**
Matthew 11:28-30, **176**
Matthew 6:26, **188**
Mark 10:8, **25**
Mark 10:9, **25**
John 17:20-26, **176**
John 19:30, **3**
John 5:19, 30, 36; 7:16; 8:28, 38; 12:49-50; 14:10, 24, **211**
Acts 16:31, **3**
Acts 5:1-9, **228**
Acts 5:2, **203**
Romans 12:1-2, **107**
Romans 12:17-21, **64**
Romans 13:1-7, **227**
Romans 3:23, **3**
Romans 5:12, **31**
Romans 5:8, **3**
Romans 6:1-14, **79**
Romans 6:12-13, **43**
Romans 6:23a, **3**
Romans 7:14-25, **77**
Romans 7:15-25, **43**
Romans 7:17, **43**
Romans 7:22, **251**

Romans 7:22-23, **252**
Romans 7:24, **77**
Romans 7:25, **78**
Romans 8:34, **176**
Romans 8:35-39, **176**
1 Corinthians 1:30, **178**
1 Corinthians 11:3, **210**, **223**
1 Corinthians 12:13, **178**
1 Corinthians 13, **172**
1 Corinthians 13:4-7, **45**
1 Corinthians 15:28, **211**
1 Corinthians 15:3-4, **3**
1 Corinthians 4:1-2, **140**
1 Corinthians 5, **114**
1 Corinthians 6:12-20, **25**
2 Corinthians 3:18, **167**
2 Corinthians 4:10-1, **168**
2 Corinthians 4:10-11, **191**, **231**
2 Corinthians 4:16, **251**, **252**
2 Corinthians 5:14, **189**
2 Corinthians 5:14-15, **261**
2 Corinthians 5:15-17, **44**
2 Corinthians 6:14, **87**
Galatians 2:20, **76**, **167**
Galatians 5:16, **46**
Galatians 5:19-21, **88**
Galatians 5:19-21a, **43**
Galatians 5:22, **79**
Galatians 5:22-23, **69**, **173**
Galatians 6:7-8, **113**
Ephesians 1:3, **179**, **209**
Ephesians 3:14-16, **251**
Ephesians 3:16, **251**

Ephesians 3:3-5, **176**
Ephesians 4:15, **53**, **54**
Ephesians 5, **76**, **203**
Ephesians 5:18, **76**, **163**, **166**, **212**
Ephesians 5:18-21, **193**
Ephesians 5:22, **76**, **160**, **214**, **230**, **238**
Ephesians 5:22-24, **212**
Ephesians 5:22-6:9, **168**
Ephesians 5:25, **76**, **143**, **160**, **161**, **163**, **193**, **194**
Ephesians 5:25-33, **143**, **170**
Ephesians 5:33, **228**, **244**
Ephesians 6:1, **227**
Ephesians 6:5, **227**
Colossians 1:26-27, **176**
Colossians 1:29, **167**
Colossians 3:16, **194**
Colossians 3:16-18, **193**
Colossians 3:18, **230**, **238**
Colossians 3:19, **193**, **194**
Colossians 3:5, **68**
1 Thessalonians 2:7, **188**
1 Timothy 1:18-20, **119**
2 Timothy 2:2, **140**
Titus 2:11-13, **56**
Titus 3:5, **181**
Hebrews 11:6, **155**
Hebrews 12:14-15, **59**
Hebrews 12:15, **198**
Hebrews 13:4, **112**
Hebrews 5:4, **203**

Scripture Index

James 1:19-20, **49**
James 1:2-4, **100**
1 Peter 2:1, **73**
1 Peter 2:18-23, **64**
1 Peter 2:21-25, **199**, **235**
1 Peter 3:1-2, **234**
1 Peter 3:1-6, **233**
1 Peter 3:7, **198**, **218**
1 John 1:9, **57**, **58**
1 John 2:14-17, **43**

ABOUT THE AUTHOR

Dr. John Thomas Clark holds his bachelor's degree in Mathematics from the University of Texas at San Antonio, has a master's degree in Theology (Th.M.) from Tyndale Theological Seminary and Biblical Institute, and his doctorate degree (DMin) with an emphasis on expository preaching from Dallas Theological Seminary. He values systematic, verse-by-verse Bible teaching and enjoys drawing out truths from the original languages.

John has served as the Senior Pastor of Grace Community Fellowship in Newnan, Georgia since September 2016. Additionally, John was a founding board member of DM2 (Disciple Makers Multiplied), a mission organization focused on pastoral training and discipleship of other disciple-makers. John still leads DM2's field to Liberia, Africa and travels there twice a year to train pastors.

John's first and foremost ministry lies in being a husband to his wife, Carrie, and a loving father to their five children. For more teaching from Pastor John Clark, please visit www.gracenewnan.org.